How to do non-verbal reasoning

Alison Primrose

Introduction

About non-verbal reasoning

This book is a step-by-step guide to all the different types of questions commonly set in non-verbal reasoning tests up to 11+ exams. It can be used on its own for practice and learning alongside any other non-verbal reasoning papers you might have. Or it may be used hand-in-hand with *Bond Assessment Papers in Non-verbal Reasoning*, which provide sets of graded papers for development and extensive practice of reasoning skills.

Non-verbal reasoning activities take many forms. The earliest activities in this book reflect questions set at an easier level and use pictures of everyday objects. The next stage introduces simple symbols, shapes and patterns, and these then become more complex as the level of difficulty increases.

How to use this book

There are three core types of reasoning which occur almost universally in non-verbal reasoning tests. The way the questions are phrased and presented however can take different forms:

Similarities
In this question type it is necessary to identify common features among a set of given pictures, objects, symbols or patterns. Question wording may require identification of the 'odd one out' or the identification of the one which would belong with a given set.

Sequences
In these questions it is necessary to find out the order, pattern or link between a set of pictures, objects, symbols or patterns. Questions may require confirmation of a repeating pattern, completion of a symmetrical grid or identification of the next step of a story or developmental progression.

Analogies
In these questions the association or link between two pictures, objects, symbols or patterns has to be identified and then applied to complete a second pair in the same way.

The range of possibilities for non-verbal reasoning questions is infinite. Also, each individual, whether child or adult, perceives shapes and patterns differently. There can therefore be no right or wrong way of tackling these questions. What this book sets out to do is to provide some tools, ideas and suggestions for tackling non-verbal reasoning questions which will ensure a careful, methodical approach and consequently greater success than through more haphazard guesswork.

The title is a brief summary of what this type is about.

At the top of the page an example of the type is given.

This explains step-by-step how to tackle the example question. It begins with a short general statement explaining how to tackle questions of this kind.

This takes you step by step through the example question, explaining the best strategy for tackling it.

This gives you further questions to try in order to build up familiarity and confidence. You will find the answers in the back.

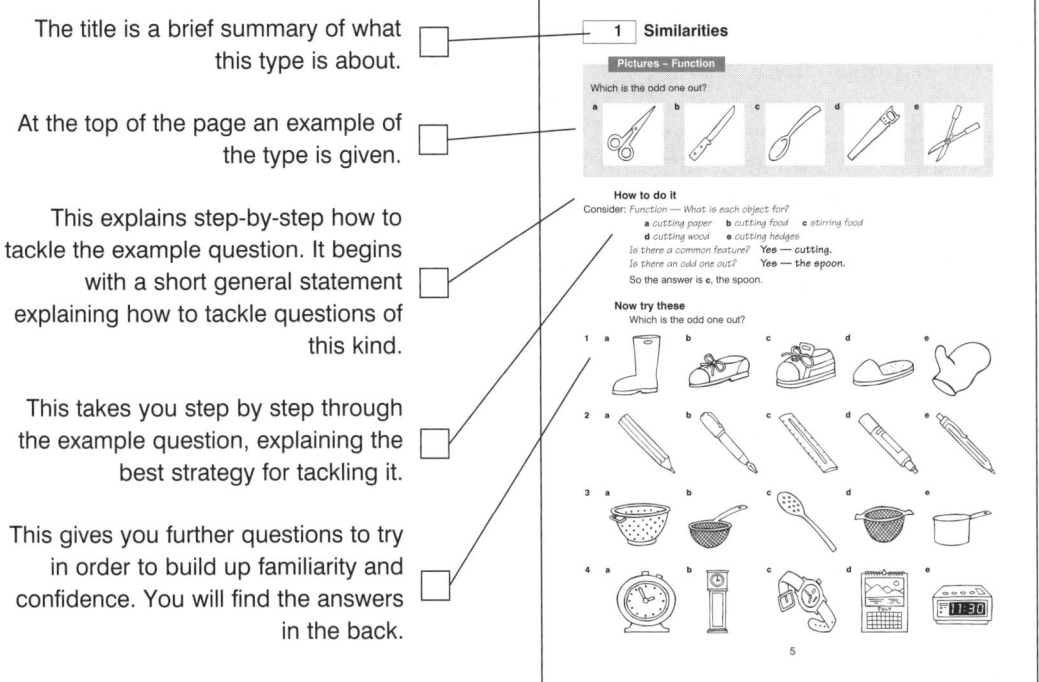

The keys to success in non-verbal reasoning

1 *Work carefully and methodically*
It is important to keep the pictures or symbols in the given order. To make sure that you have not missed or muddled any options, always work from left to right, identifying the features of each symbol or picture as you go.

2 *Use your pencil to help 'match up' or eliminate options*
Don't be afraid of making notes or marks by the questions. It is often helpful to cross out options that you have eliminated as answers. Put a single line through the symbol so that it is still visible. Drawing arrows or lines can help when trying to match elements of a pattern, or when finding rotations or translations of shapes.

3 *Inspect the shapes, patterns or symbols very carefully*
Non-verbal reasoning involves a lot of detail and quite small pictures — make sure you look very hard at each picture or symbol so that you notice every feature.

4 *Consider all the possible variables*
Make sure you have checked all of the features of each picture or symbol. Use the list to help you remember.

For many types of non-verbal reasoning question there is no clear 'right' or 'wrong' classification. The following checklist will help to ensure that you consider and notice all possible variables:

Shape – what shape is each picture or symbol?
Position – are the pictures in similar or different positions?
Angle – are the pictures at particular angles?
Number – how many objects or features are in each picture or symbol?
Shading – is there any change or consistency to the shading?
Size – does the size of each picture or symbol change or remain the same?

Learn this list!

Here are some suggestions of ways to remember '**SPANSS**':

Some **P**eople **A**re **N**ot **S**o **S**illy!

Spotty **P**yjamas **A**nd **N**ice **S**oft **S**lippers

You may like to make up one of your own. Write it here and learn it:

S	**S**hape
P	**P**osition
A	**A**ngle
N	**N**umber
S	**S**hading
S	**S**ize

The only exceptions to this rule are questions that use pictures of everyday objects or situations rather than shapes or patterns. For these you may need to consider the questions:

What are they for? Function
Where are they found? Location

This book is set out giving examples in all the different categories considering the different variables in turn.

1 | Similarities

Which is the odd one out?

a 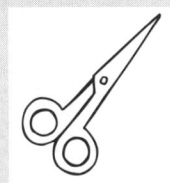　b 　c 　d 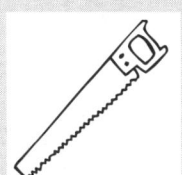　e

How to do it

Consider: *Function — What is each object for?*

    a *cutting paper*　**b** *cutting food*　**c** *stirring food*

    d *cutting wood*　**e** *cutting hedges*

    Is there a common feature? **Yes — cutting.**

    Is there an odd one out? **Yes — the spoon.**

So the answer is **c**, the spoon.

Now try these

Which is the odd one out?

1　a 　b 　c 　d 　e

2　a 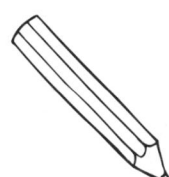　b 　c 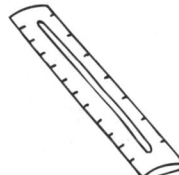　d 　e

3　a 　b 　c 　d 　e

4　a 　b 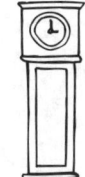　c 　d 　e

2 Similarities

Which is the odd one out?

a  b 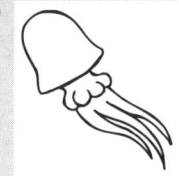 c  d 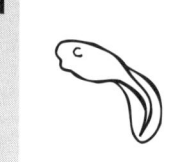 e

How to do it

Consider: *Function — What is each object for?* **Nothing.**

Location — Where is each object found?

a *in water* **b** *in water* **c** *in the air* **d** *in water* **e** *in water*

Is there a common feature? **Yes, water.**

Is there an odd one out? **Yes, the dragonfly.**

So the answer is **c**, the dragonfly.

Now try these

Which is the odd one out?

1 a 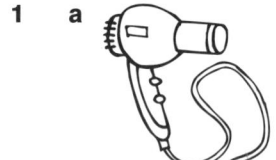 b  c 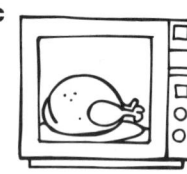 d  e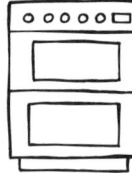

2 a  b  c  d  e

3 a  b  c  d  e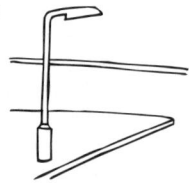

4 a  b  c  d  e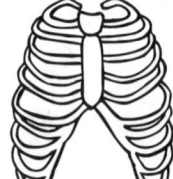

3 | Similarities

Which is the odd one out?

a    b    c    d    e

How to do it

Consider: *Function — What is each object for?*

Look at what each sign means:

> **a** *pedestrian crossing*   **b** *slippery road*   **c** *no entry*
> **d** *traffic lights*   **e** *priority over oncoming traffic*

All of the signs mean different things.

So there is no odd one out.

Location — Where is each object found?

Think where you would find each object:

> **a** *near a pedestrian crossing*   **b** *where the road is slippery*
> **c** *at a one way street*   **d** *near traffic lights*
> **e** *where you have priority on a road*

All of the signs are found near the road.

So there is no odd one out.

So now use SPANSS

Shape — What shapes make up each sign?

Look at the shapes inside the signs:

> **a** *a man and two lines*   **b** *two bendy lines and a car*   **c** *a rectangle*
> **d** *three circles*   **e** *two arrows*

All of the shapes inside the signs are different.

So there is no odd one out.

Look at the outside shapes of the signs:

> **a** *triangle*   **b** *triangle*   **c** *circle*   **d** *triangle*   **e** *triangle*

All of the signs are triangular apart from **c**, which is a circle.

So **c** is the odd one out.

Now check there are no other variables that could give answers.

Is there an odd one out in terms of:

Position — **no.**	*Angle* — **no.**
Number — **no.**	*Shading* — **no.**
Size — **no.**	

So the answer is **c**.

Now try these

Which is the odd one out?

4 | Similarities

Which is the odd one out?

a  b  c  d  e

How to do it

Consider: *Function — What is each object for?*

The pictures are all houses.

So there is no odd one out.

Location — Where would you find each object?

The pictures are all houses.

So there is no odd one out.

Shape — What shapes make up each object?

**All the shapes are the same (the outline of a house)
and contain the three square windows and one rectangular door.**

So there is no odd one out.

Position — What are the positions of the windows and doors in each house?

Look at the positions of the windows and doors:

**All the windows and doors are in the same position apart from e,
which has its door on the left.**

So **e** is the odd one out.

Now check there are no other variables that could give answers.

Is there an odd one out in terms of:

Angle — **no.**

Number — **no.**

Shading — **no.**

Size — **no.**

So the answer is **e**.

Now try these

Which is the odd one out?

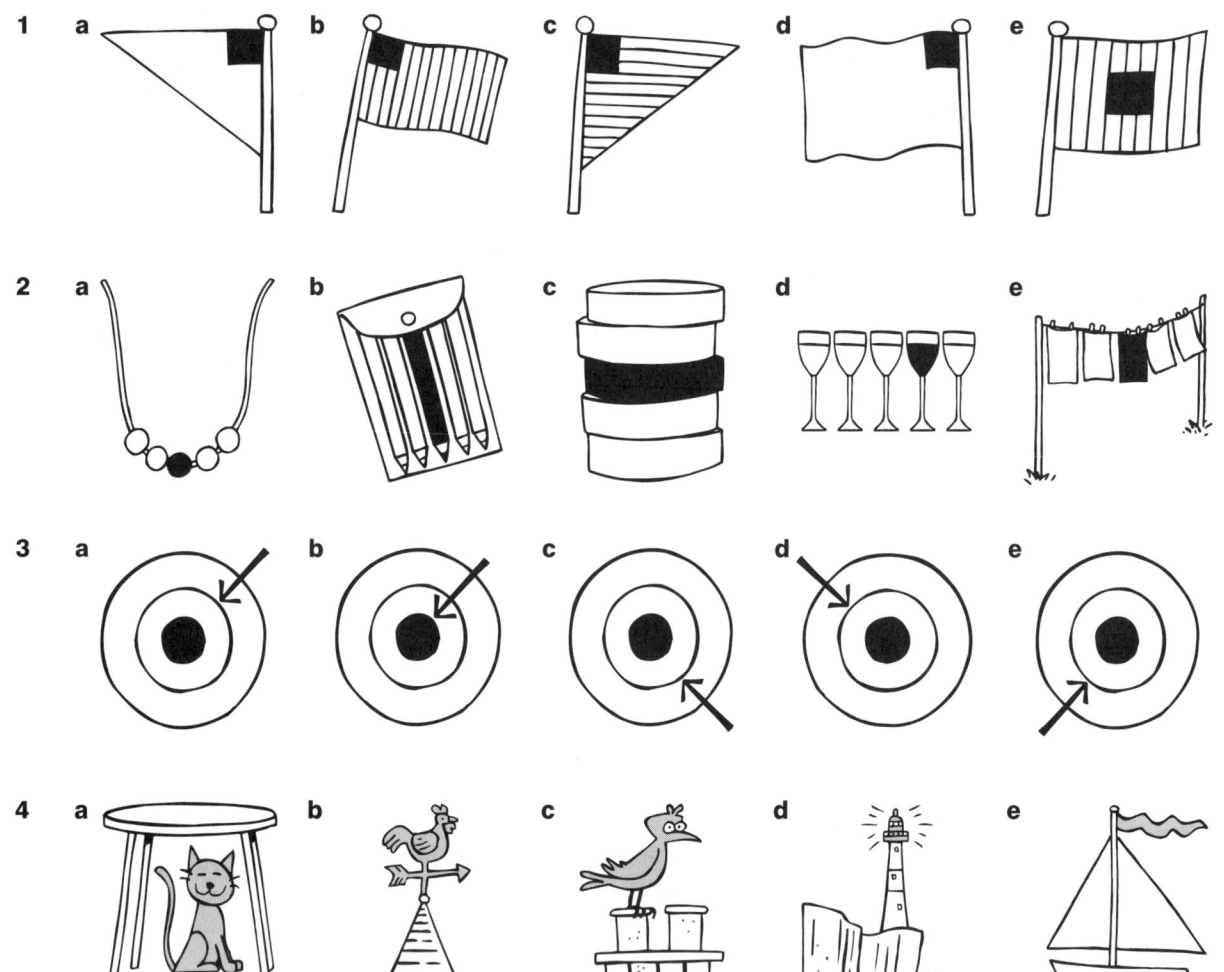

Pictures – Angle

Which is the odd one out?

a  b  c  d  e

How to do it

Consider: *Function — What does each object do?*
The objects are all clock faces.
So there is no odd one out.

Location — Where would you find each object?
The objects are all clock faces.
So there is no odd one out.

Shape — What shape is each object?
Look at the inside shapes and the outline shapes:
The inside shapes are always two arrows.
The outline shapes are always circles.
So there is no odd one out.

Position — What is the position of each object?
Look at the positions of the inside shapes and the outline shapes:
The circles are all in the same position.
The arrows are all in different positions, and are all fixed in the centre.

So there is no odd one out.

Angle — What are the angles in each picture?
Look at each angle:
   a right angle (*90°*)   **b** right angle (*90°*)   **c** right angle (*90°*)
   d less than a right angle (*30°*)   **e** right angle (*90°*)
The arrows are always at right angles to each other apart from
the arrows in d, which are at less than a right angle (30°) to each other.
So **d** is the odd one out.

Now check there are no other variables that could give answers.
Is there an odd one out in terms of:
Number — **no.**   **S**hading — **no.**   **S**ize — **no.**
So the answer is **d**.

Now try these

Which is the odd one out?

6 Similarities

Which is the odd one out?

a  b  c  d  e

How to do it

Consider: *Function — What does each object do?*
The objects are all flowers.

So there is no odd one out.

Location — Where would you find each object?
The objects are all flowers.

So there is no odd one out.

Shape — What shape is each object?
All the outline shapes are flowers.
Some petals are narrower than others.

So there is no odd one out.

Position — What is the position of each flower?
All the flowers are in the same position.
All the petals are in similar positions.

So there is no odd one out.

Angle — Are the flowers in certain rotational positions?
There is no regular pattern to the rotation of the flowers.

So there is no odd one out.

Number — How many petals are there on each flower?
    a 5   **b** 5   **c** 6   **d** 5   **e** 5
The flowers all have 5 petals apart from c, which has 6.

So **c** is the odd one out.

Now check there are no other variables that could give answers.

Is there an odd one out in terms of:
Shading — **no.**
Size — **no.**

So the answer is **c**.

Now try these

Which is the odd one out?

Pictures – Shading

Which is the odd one out?

a    b    c    d    e

How to do it

Consider: *Function — What are the objects for?*
All the objects are snowmen.

So there is no odd one out.

Location — Where would you find each object?
All the objects are snowmen.

So there is no odd one out.

Shape — What shape are the objects?
Look at the outline shapes.
All the shapes are the same — they are all snowmen.

So there is no odd one out.

Look at the individual parts of each shape.
All the snowmen have a similarly-shaped hat and scarf.

So there is no odd one out.

Position — What is the position of the parts of each snowman?
Look at the hat and scarf.
All the hats and scarves are in similar positions.

So there is no odd one out.

Angle — Are the snowmen or their clothes rotated or at an angle?
Look at the snowmen and their hats and scarves.
There is no rotation in the pictures.

So there is no odd one out.

Shading — Are there any patterns in the shading?
Look at the snowmen:
The snowmen are all white.

So there is no odd one out.

Look at the hats and scarves:

	a	**b**	**c**	**d**	**e**
hat	grey	striped	grey	grey	grey
scarf	striped	grey	striped	striped	striped

They all have grey hats and striped scarves except for **b**, which has a striped hat and a grey scarf.

So **b** is the odd one out.

Is there an odd one out in terms of:

Size — **no.**

So the answer is **b**.

Now try these

Which is the odd one out?

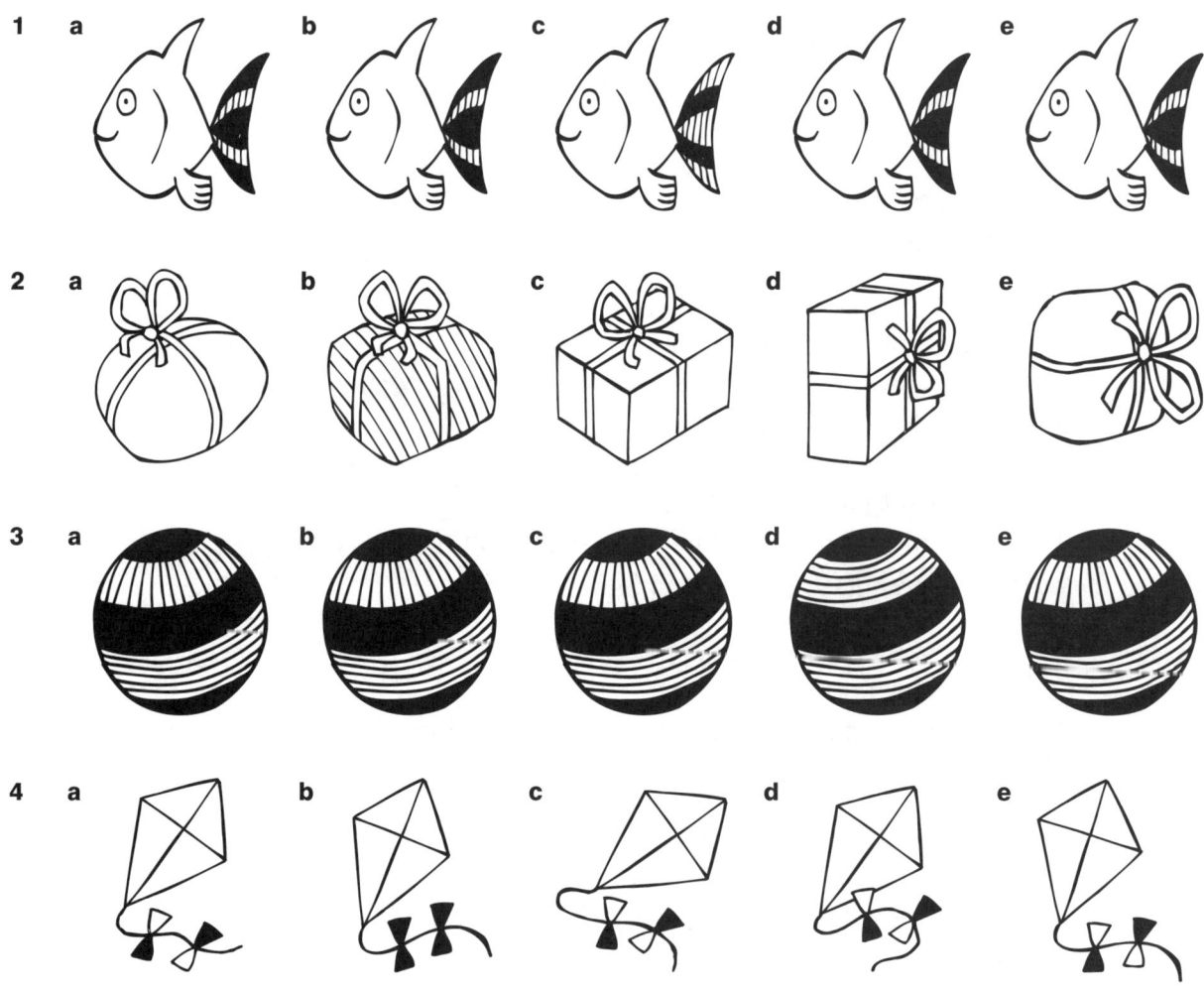

Which is the odd one out?

a  b  c  d  e

How to do it

Consider: *Function — What does each object do?*

All the objects are trees.

So there is no odd one out.

Location — Where would you find each object?

They are all found in forests. Some might be found in different sorts of location but there is no clear pattern.

So there is no odd one out.

Shape — What shape is each object?

Look at the trees.

The trees are all different shapes.

So there is no odd one out.

Position — What is the position of each tree?

Look at the branches.

Some have visible branches and some do not.

There is no pattern to the positions of the branches.

So there is no odd one out.

Angle — What angles are involved in each tree?

Look at the trees.

All of the trees are standing up apart from d.

Look at the branches.

The branches are at different angles, but two trees have no visible branches.

So **d** could be the odd one out.

Number — What numbers are involved in each tree?

Look at the branches.

The first two trees have no branches, two have two main branches and one (d) is just branches, and is not a complete tree.

So **d** could be the odd one out.

Shading — What is the shading of each tree?

Look at the leaves of the trees.

There is no shading.

So there is no odd one out.

Size — What is the size of each tree?

Look at the trees.

    a *a normal-sized tree*   **b** *could be a Christmas tree or a big pine tree*

    c *looks like a normal tree*   **d** *a branch of a tree*   **e** *looks like a smallish tree*

The trees are all of different sizes, but d is just a branch.

A branch is smaller than a tree because a branch is part of a tree.

So **d** is the odd one out.

There are no other variables to check.

So the answer is **d**.

Now try these

Which is the odd one out?

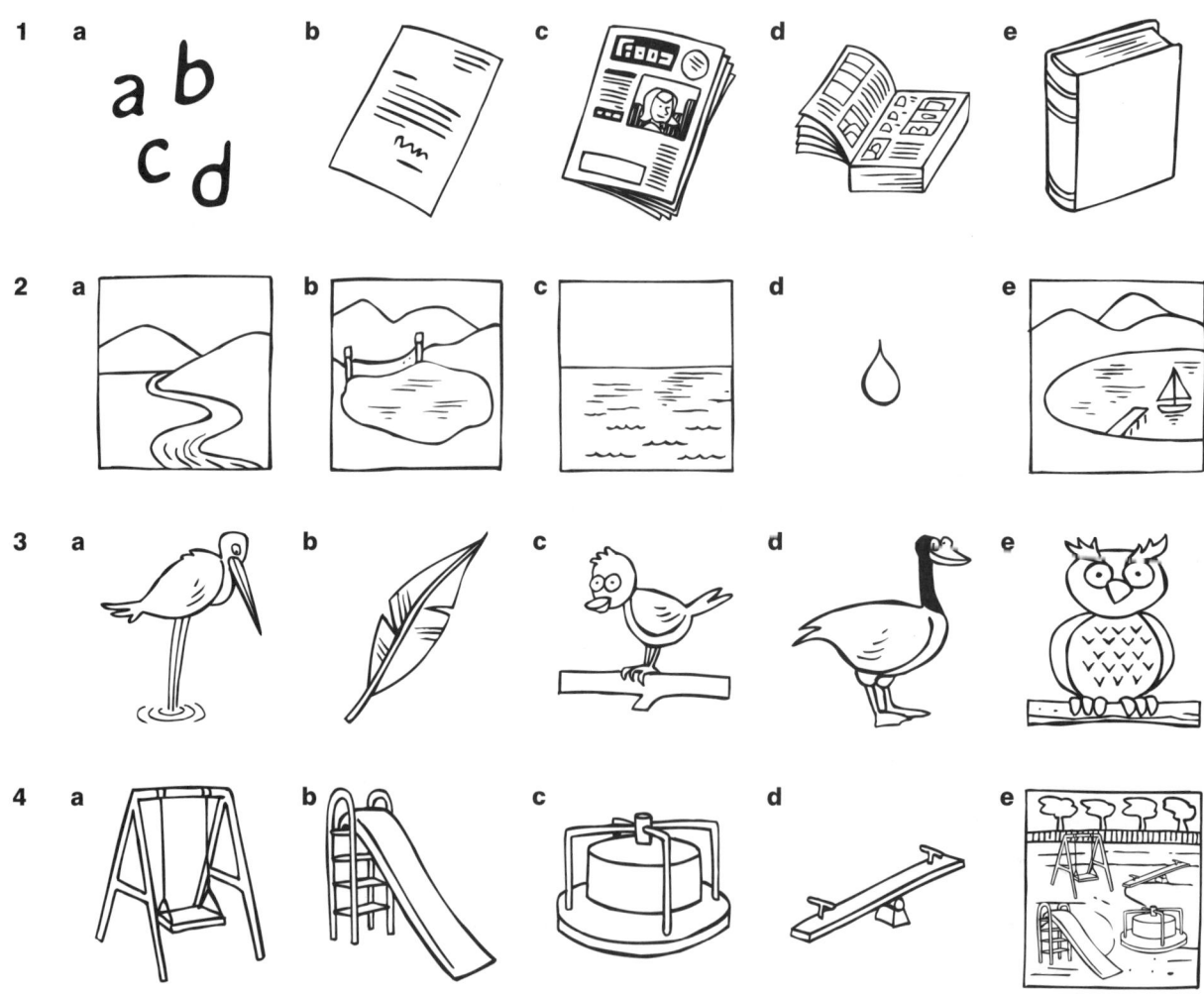

18

Which one comes next?

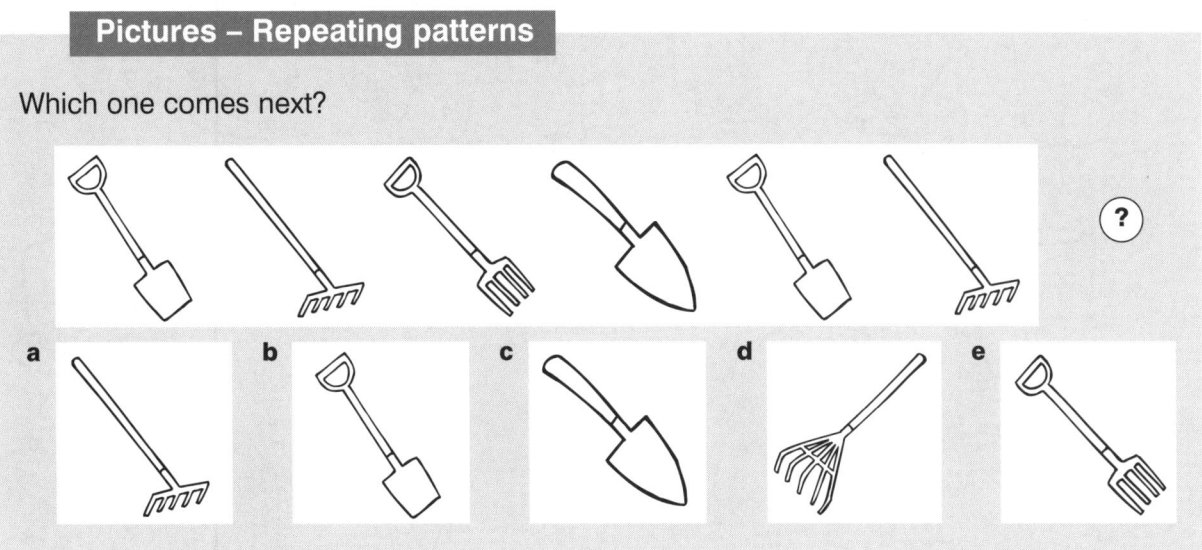

How to do it

Some patterns do not quite fit into the normal **SPANSS** formula. This is because they are repeating patterns. In each repeating pattern there is a block of symbols or pictures that repeats itself exactly. Look for this sort of pattern first of all, before you use **SPANSS**.

Look carefully at the pictures.
Does the first picture reappear in the sequence?
The first picture, the spade, is also the fifth picture.
Does the second picture reappear in the sequence?
The second picture, the rake, is also the sixth picture.
So there is a repeating pattern.

Underline the section that makes up the repeating block in the pattern.

Now match the objects one by one so that you can see which shape should repeat itself next and continue the pattern.
The seventh shape should be the same as the third shape, the fork.
So the answer is **e**.

19

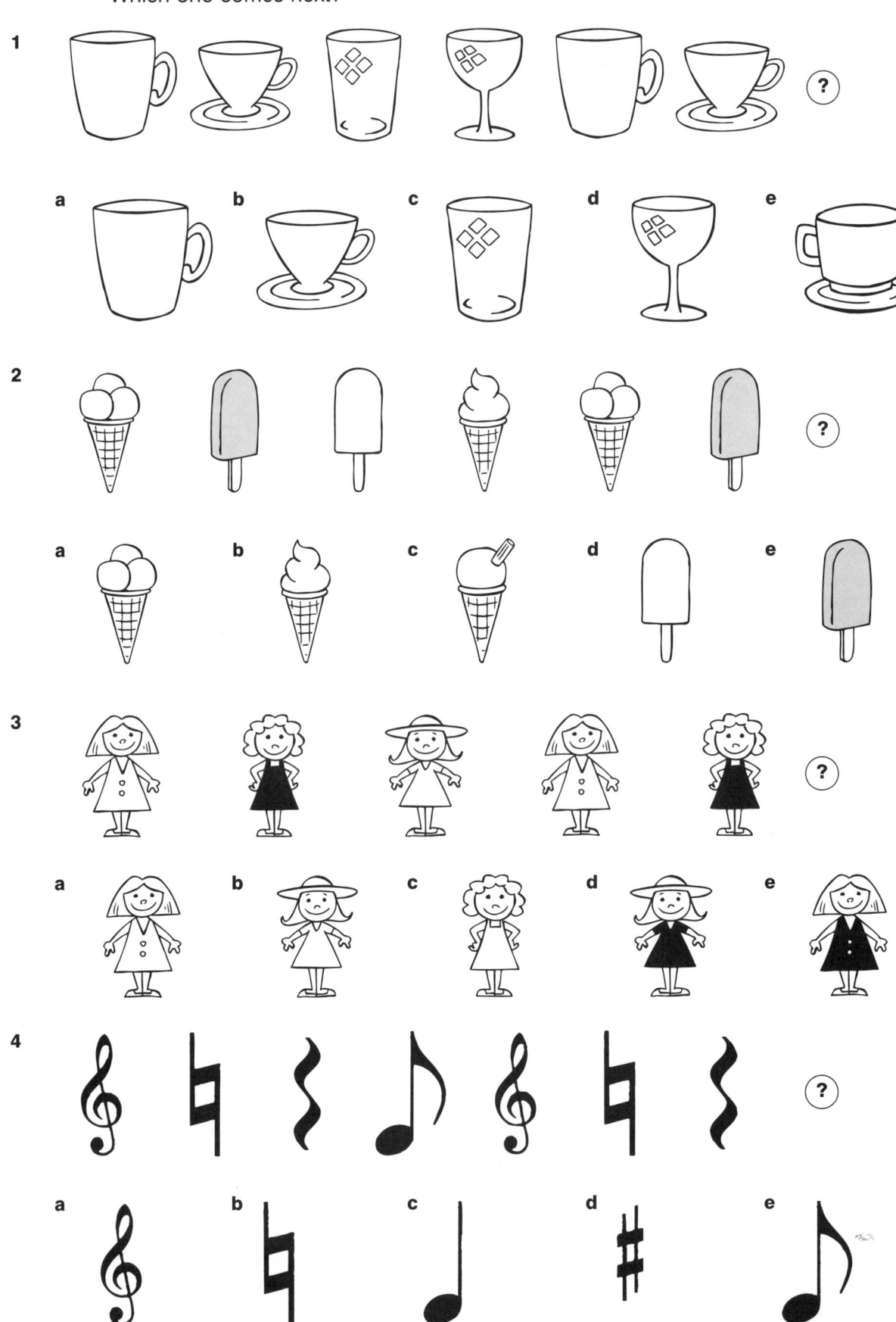

10 Sequences

Which one comes next?

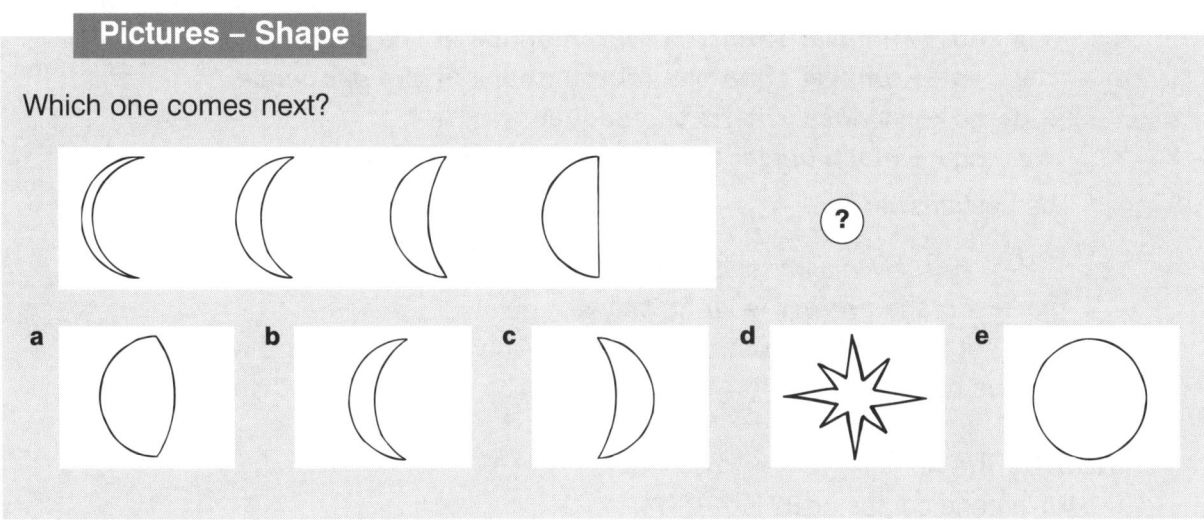

How to do it

Consider: *Repeating pattern — Does the first picture reappear in the pattern?* **No.**

So it is not a repeating pattern.

Shape — Do the shapes change in a regular way?
Look at the shapes and how they change.
Each shape is bigger than the one before it.
The line on the right hand side of the shape moves across,
while the line on the left hand side remains the same.

Now you know how the shapes are changing, work through the possible answers
checking to see if one of them would be the next shape in the sequence.

For this sequence, you are looking for a shape where the left hand line is the same,
and the right hand line is one stage further across.

	left side the same?	*right side one stage further across?*
a	yes	yes
b	yes	no — not as far
c	no — further across	no — more than one stage further across
d	no — it's star-shaped	no — it's star-shaped
e	yes	no — more than one stage further across

So **a** is the next shape in the sequence.

Now check there are no other variables that could give answers.

Is there a regular sequence in terms of:

Position — no.
Angle — no.
Number — no.
Shading — no.
Size — yes, the shapes are getting bigger.

21

Check through the possible answers.

is it the next biggest in the sequence?

a   probably — slightly bigger than the fourth shape in the sequence

b   no — smaller than the fourth shape in the sequence

c   no — smaller than the fourth shape in the sequence

d   no — it does not fit the sequence

e   no — much bigger than the fourth shape in the sequence

The best answer is **a**.

Is this the same answer that you got above?

Yes — so the answer is definitely a.

If it is not the same answer, check both again very carefully and work out which is correct.

Now try these

Which one comes next?

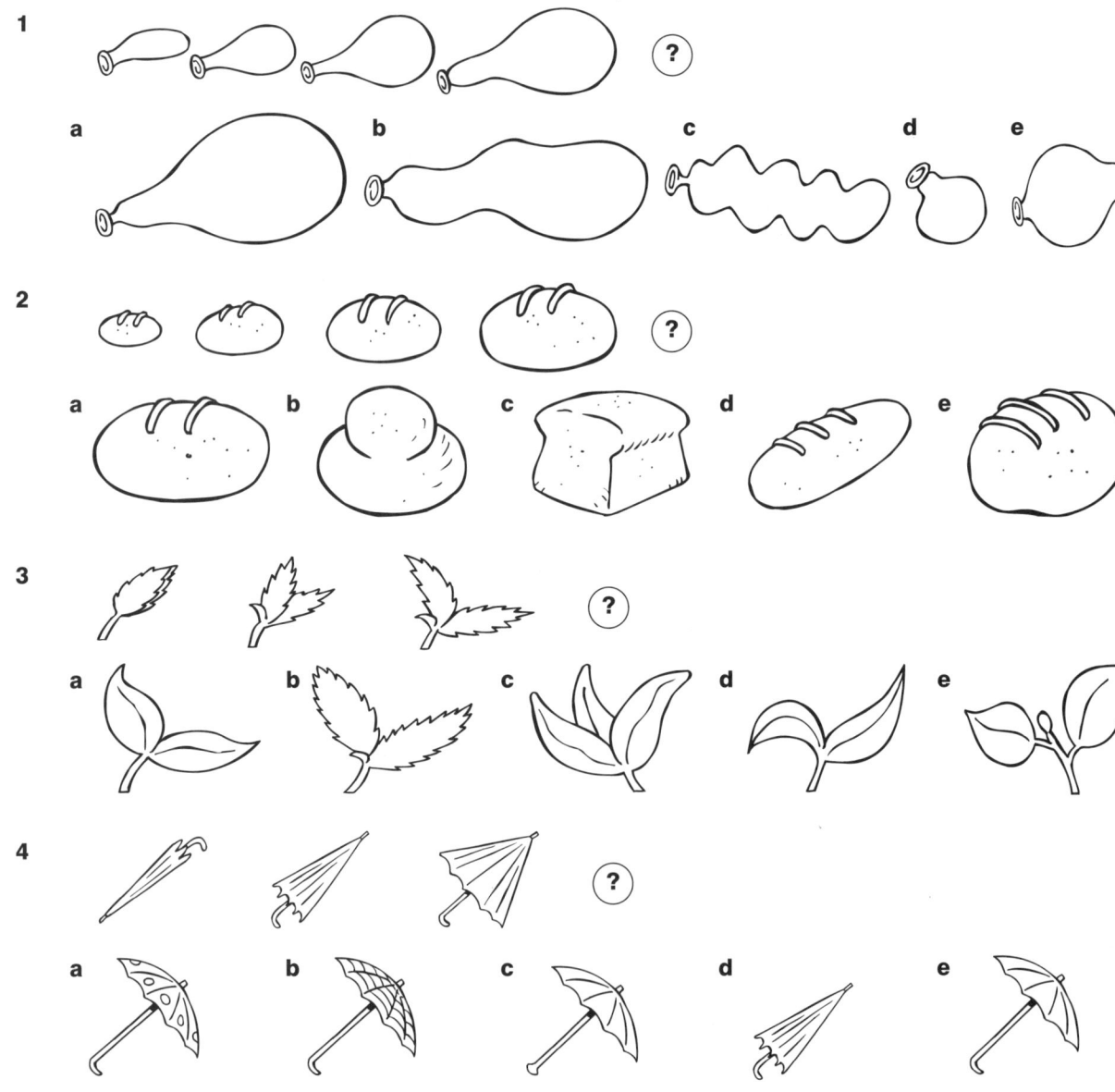

11 Sequences

Which one comes next?

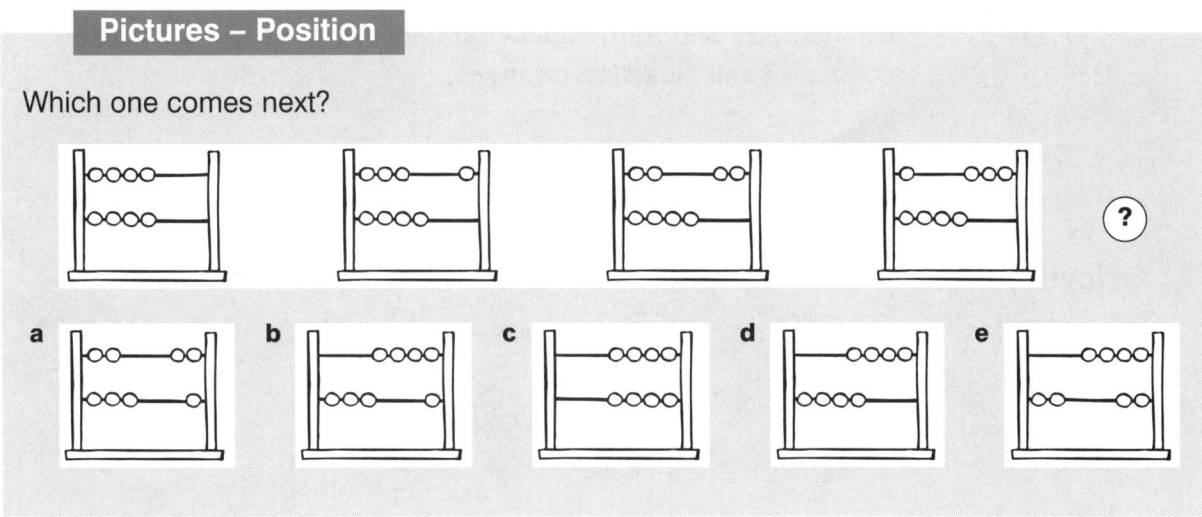

How to do it

Consider: *Repeating pattern — Does the first picture reappear in the pattern?* **No.**

So it is not a repeating pattern.

Shape — Do the outline or inside shapes change?
Look at the abacuses.
The frames stay the same, and the beads move but they don't change shape.

So there is not a regular sequence of shape.

Position — Does the position of any part or the whole change?
Look at the frames.
The frames stay in the same position.
Look at the beads.
The beads on the top row move progressively to the right.
The beads on the second row stay in the same place.

Now work through the possible answers to find a picture with one more bead on the right side of the first row (four beads) and one less bead on the left side of the first row (no beads), and with the beads on the second row remaining the same.

	none on the left?	four on the right?	second row the same?
a	no — two	no — two	no
b	yes	yes	no
c	yes	yes	no
d	yes	yes	yes
e	yes	yes	no

So **d** is the next picture in the sequence.

Now check there are no other variables that could give answers.

Is there a regular sequence in terms of:

Angle — **no.**

Number — **no, there are the same total number of beads on each frame although their position changes.**

Shading — **no.**

Size — **no.**

So the answer is **d**.

Now try these

Which one comes next?

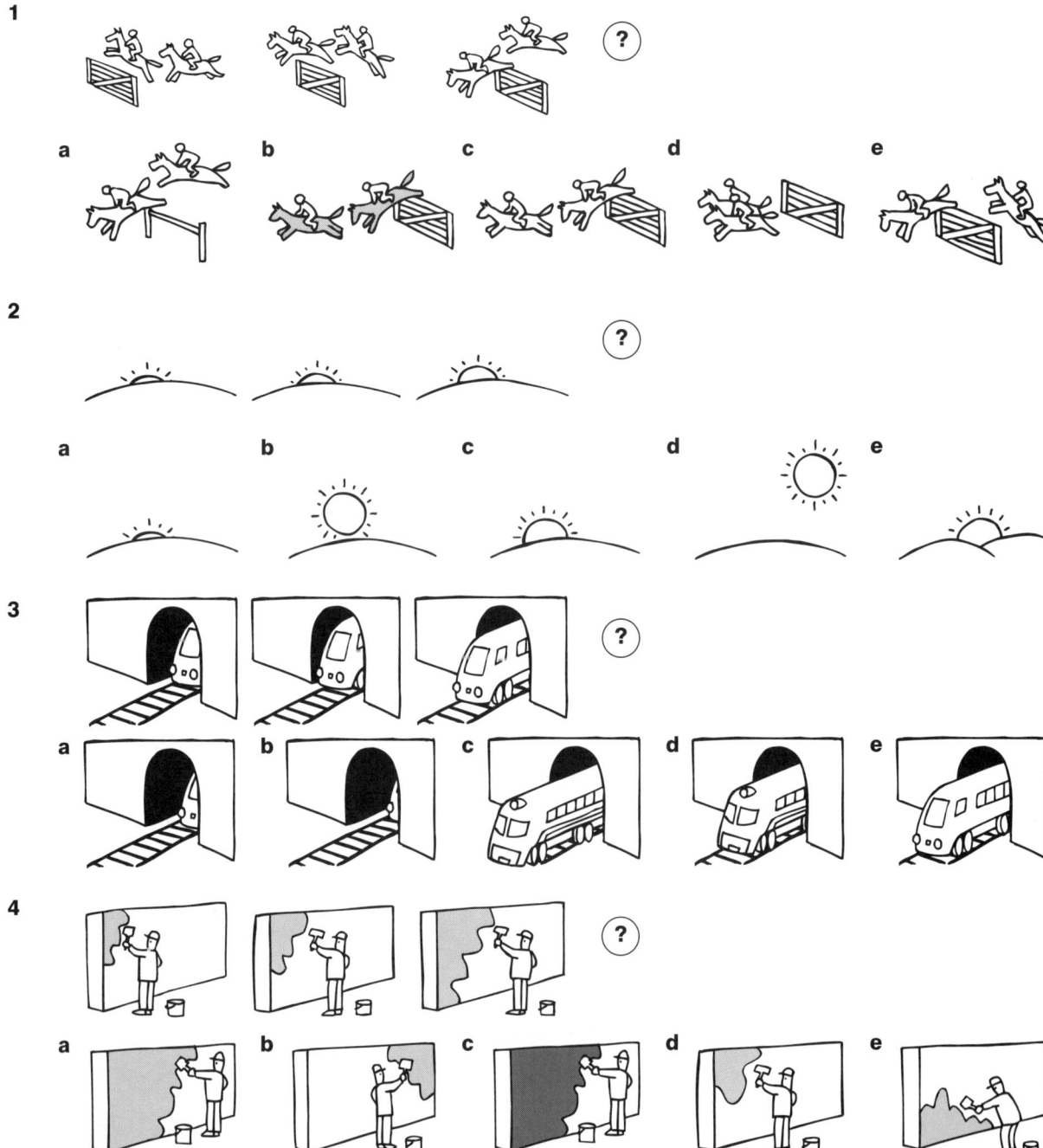

Pictures – Angle

Which one comes next?

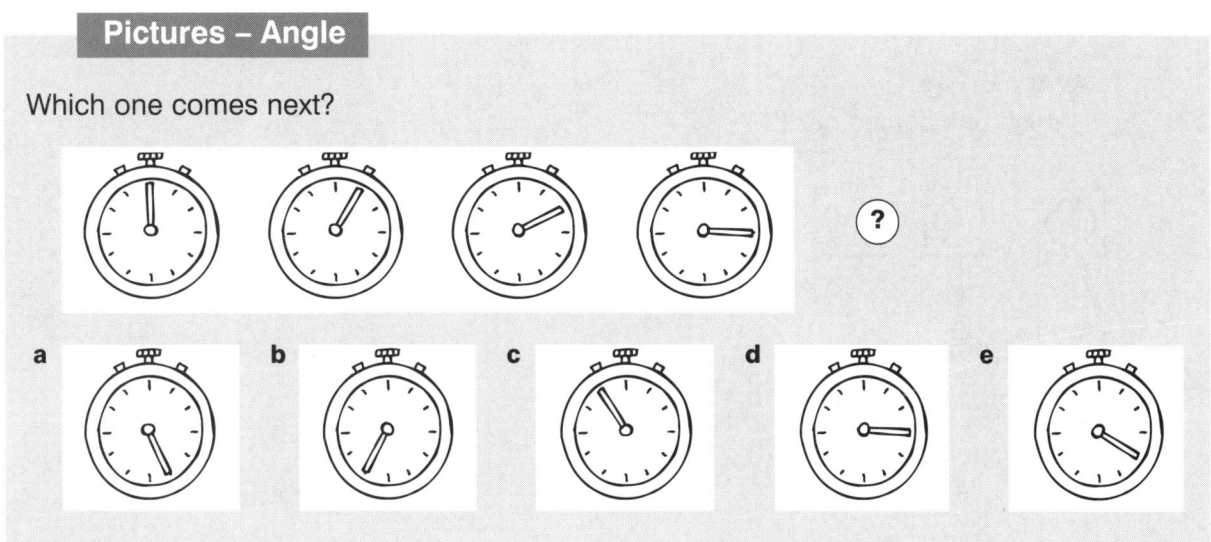

How to do it

Consider: *Repeating pattern — Does the first picture reappear in the pattern?* **No.**

So it is not a repeating pattern.

Shape — Do the shapes change in a regular way?
Look at the stopwatches.
All the stopwatches are the same shape. They each have a single hand.

So there is not a regular sequence of shape.

Position — Does the position of any of the parts change?
Look at the hands.
The hand of each stopwatch is in a different position.

So there is a sequence related to position.

Now think about what sort of position change there is.

Angle — Is the change in position related to angle?
Look at the position of the hand on each stopwatch.
The line moves clockwise through one section, 30°, each time.
So work through the possible answers to find the stopwatch where the hand is 30°, or one section, further clockwise.

    a *2 sections further*   **b** *4 sections further*   **c** *4 sections back*
    d *same position*   **e** *1 section further*

So the answer is **e**, one section or 30° further clockwise.

Now check there are no other variables that could give answers.

Is there a regular sequence in terms of:
Number   *No* **— unless you think about a clock, and then the sequence**
         above would be *12 o'clock, 1 o'clock, 2 o'clock, 3 o'clock,*
         and you need to look for *4 o'clock.*

Check that this gives the same answer. **Yes, the answer is still e.**

Shading — **no.**
Size — **no.**

Now try these

Which one comes next?

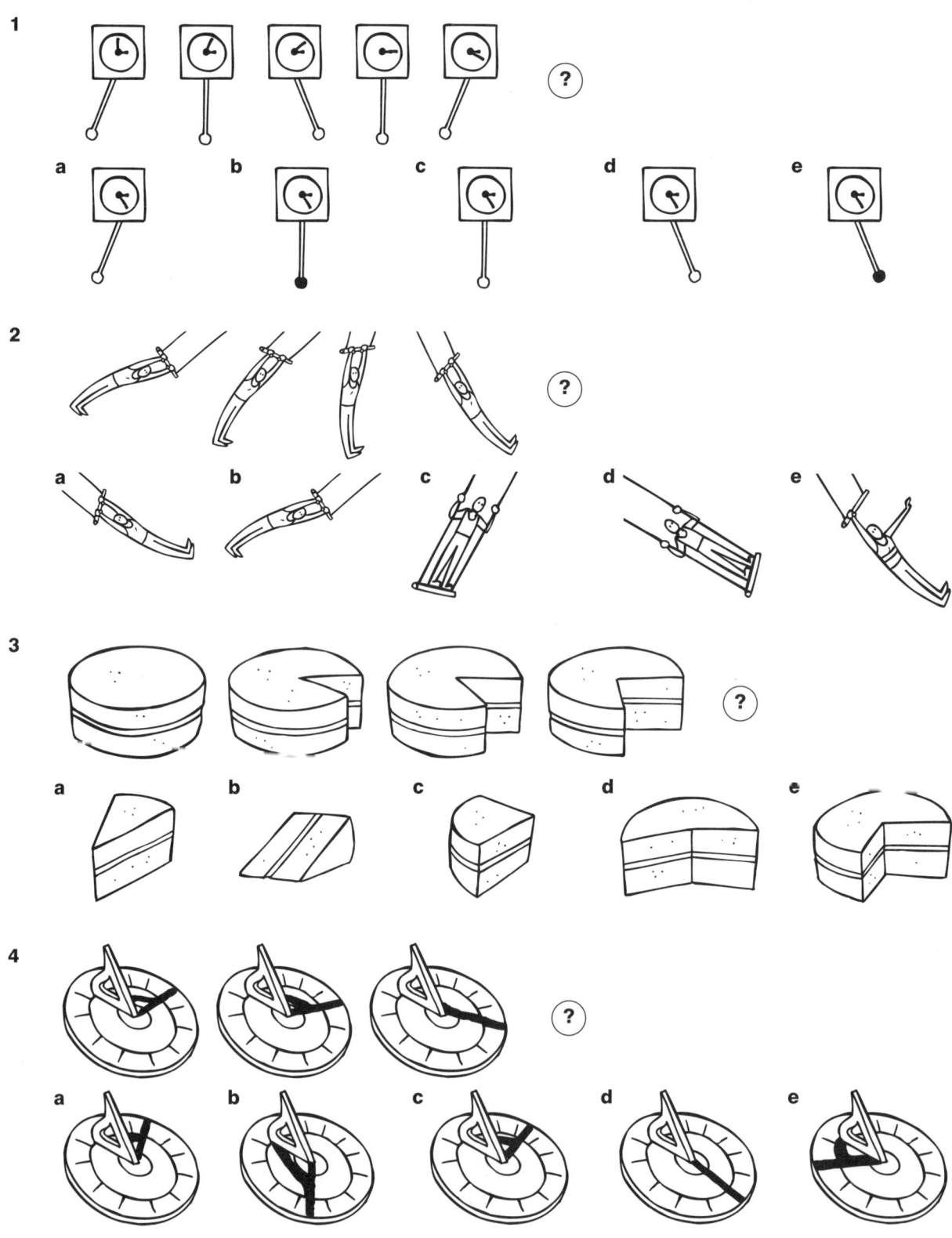

Pictures – Number

Which one comes next?

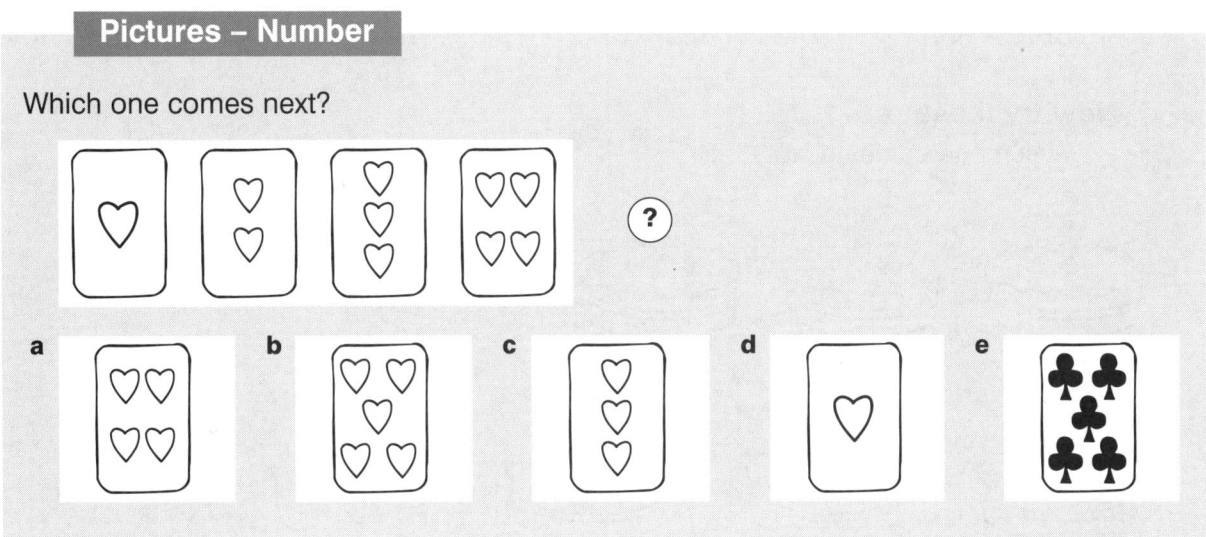

How to do it

Consider: *Repeating pattern — Does the first picture reappear in the pattern?* **No.**

So it is not a repeating pattern.

Shape — Do the shapes change in a regular way?

Look at the playing cards.

Each playing card is the same shape. They all have hearts on, but different numbers of hearts.

So the shapes do not change. The next card in the sequence must also have hearts on it.

Position — Does the position of the parts change?

Look at the hearts.

The positions of the hearts changes, but not in a regular way.

The next card in the sequence might have hearts arranged in a different way.

Angle — Do the pictures or parts rotate?

Look at the playing cards.

There is no pattern of rotation to the hearts or the playing cards.

Number — Does the number of parts change?

Count the hearts on the cards.

There is one more heart on each card on the sequence.

Look through the possible answers for a card with 5 hearts.

>   *5 hearts?*
> **a**   no — 4 hearts
> **b**   yes
> **c**   no — 3 hearts
> **d**   no — 1 heart
> **e**   no — there are 5 objects, but they are clubs, and we are looking for hearts

So the answer is **b**, 5 hearts.

27

Now check there are no other variables that could give answers.

Is there a regular sequence in terms of:

Shading — **no.**

Size — **no.**

Now try these

Which one comes next?

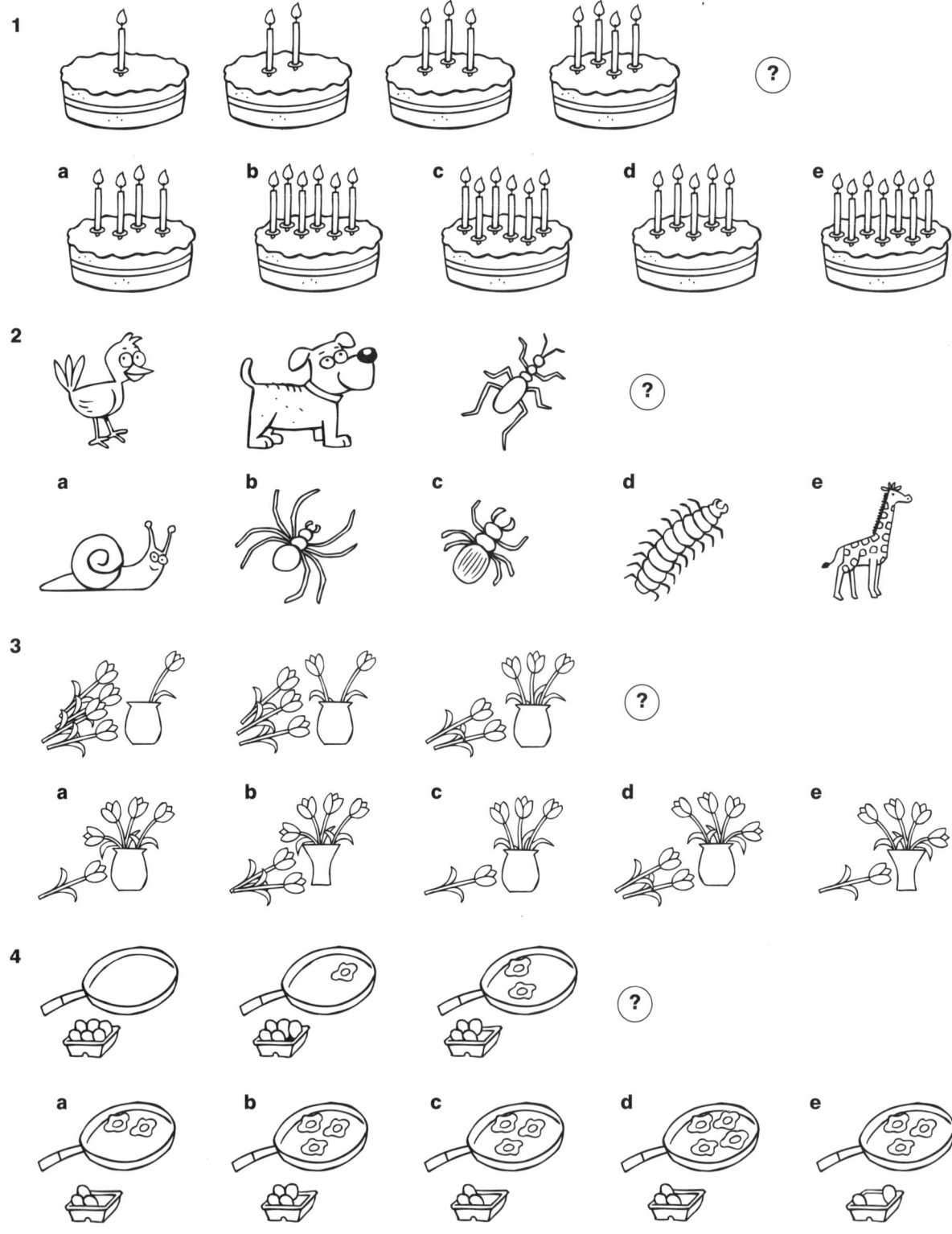

14 Sequences

Which one comes next?

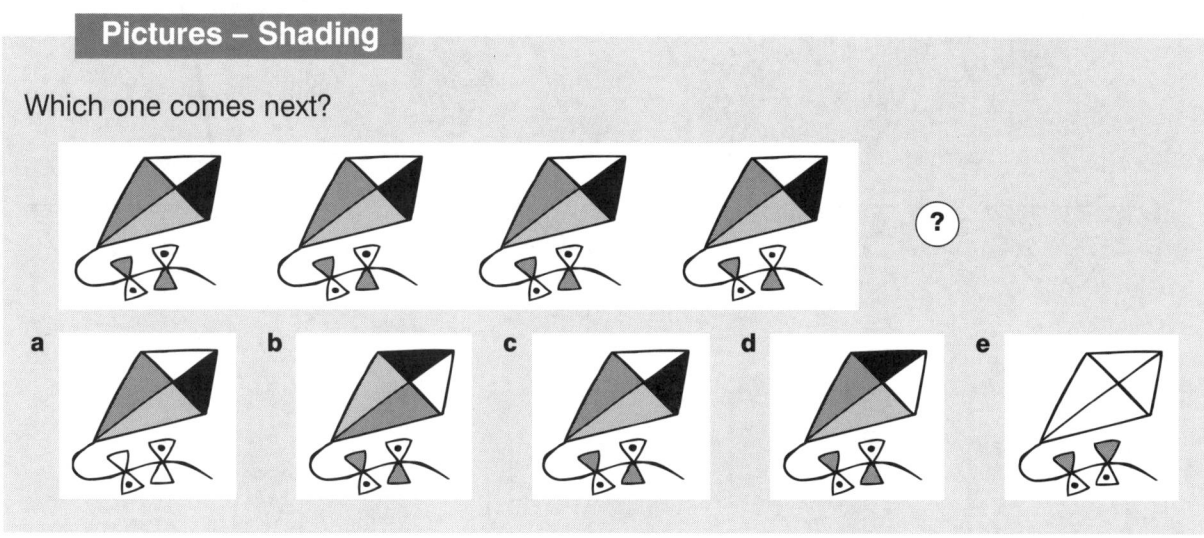

How to do it

Consider: *Repeating pattern — Does the first picture reappear in the pattern?* **Yes.**

Look at the kites — they are all the same!

The sequence is a line of identical pictures.

The next in the sequence must be exactly the same as the others.

Work through the possible answers making sure they are the same for **SPANSS**.

Shape — All the possible answers are the same shape.

Position — All the parts of each shape are in the same position.

Angle — All the kites are at the same angle.

Number — There is the same number of parts on each possible answer.

Shading — Each possible answer is shaded differently.
Work through each one checking to see if it matches the shading in the kites in the sequence.

   a two of the bows in the tail are not shaded

   b the shaded panels in the kite are the wrong way around

   c the shading matches the sequence

   d the shaded panels in the kite are different

   e the kite is not shaded at all

So the answer is **c**.

Size — All the possible answers are the same size.

So the answer is **c**.

Now try these

Which one comes next?

1

a 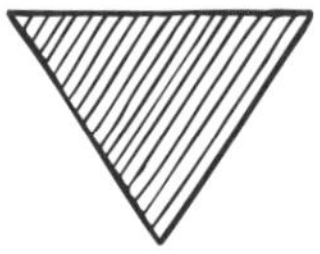   b 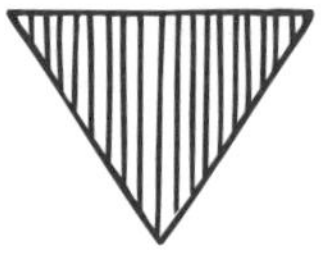   c 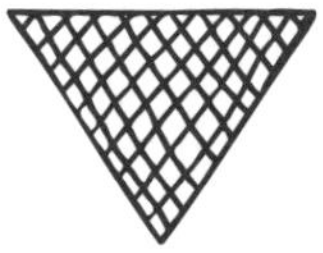   d 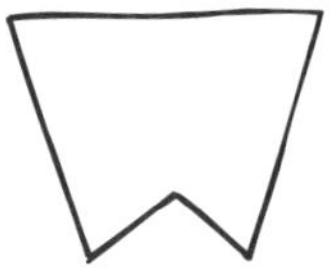   e

2

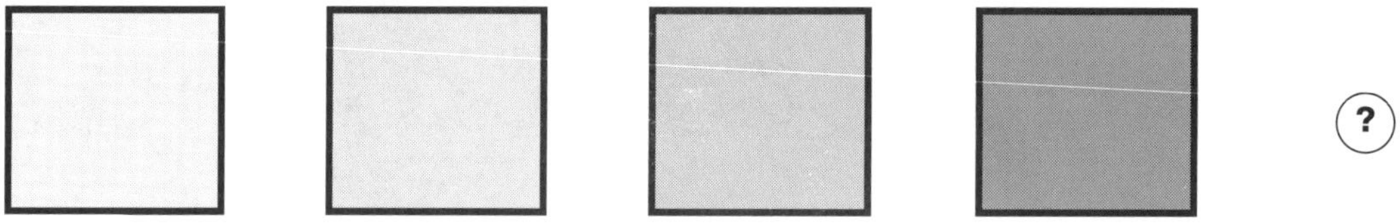

a   b   c   d    e

3

a    b    c    d    e

4

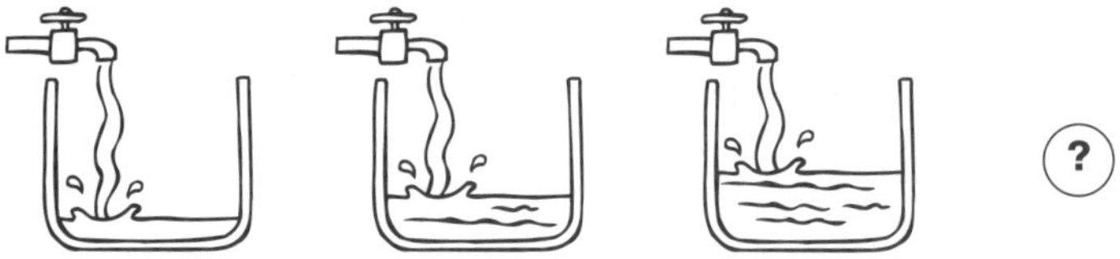

a    b    c    d    e

30

15 | Sequences

Which one comes next?

How to do it

Consider: *Repeating pattern — Does the first picture reappear in the pattern?* **No.**

So it is not a repeating pattern.

Shape — is there a regular pattern to the shapes of the objects?
The objects are all different animals.

There is no regular shape pattern.

Position — are the objects in different positions?

There is no pattern to the positions of the objects.

Angle — is there a pattern to the angles of the animals?
The animals are all at different angles.

There is no regular pattern to their angles.

Number — are there any number patterns to the animals?
The first animal has 8 legs, and the others have 4 legs.

There is no number pattern to the animals.

Shading — are the animals shaded differently?
There is no pattern to the shading of the animals.

Size — are the pictures different sizes?
There is no pattern to the sizes of the pictures — some are different sizes to others but there is no regular pattern.

Look at the animals in the pictures.
The animals get bigger as the sequence progresses. A mouse is bigger than a spider, a rabbit is bigger than a mouse and a lion is bigger than a rabbit. So even though the pictures are similar sizes, the animals are getting bigger. So we are looking for a picture of an animal bigger than a lion.

Work through the possible answers.

bigger than a lion?

    a no, much smaller

    b no, smaller

    c no, much smaller

    d yes, much bigger

    e no, much smaller

So the answer is **d**, the elephant.

Now try these

Which one comes next?

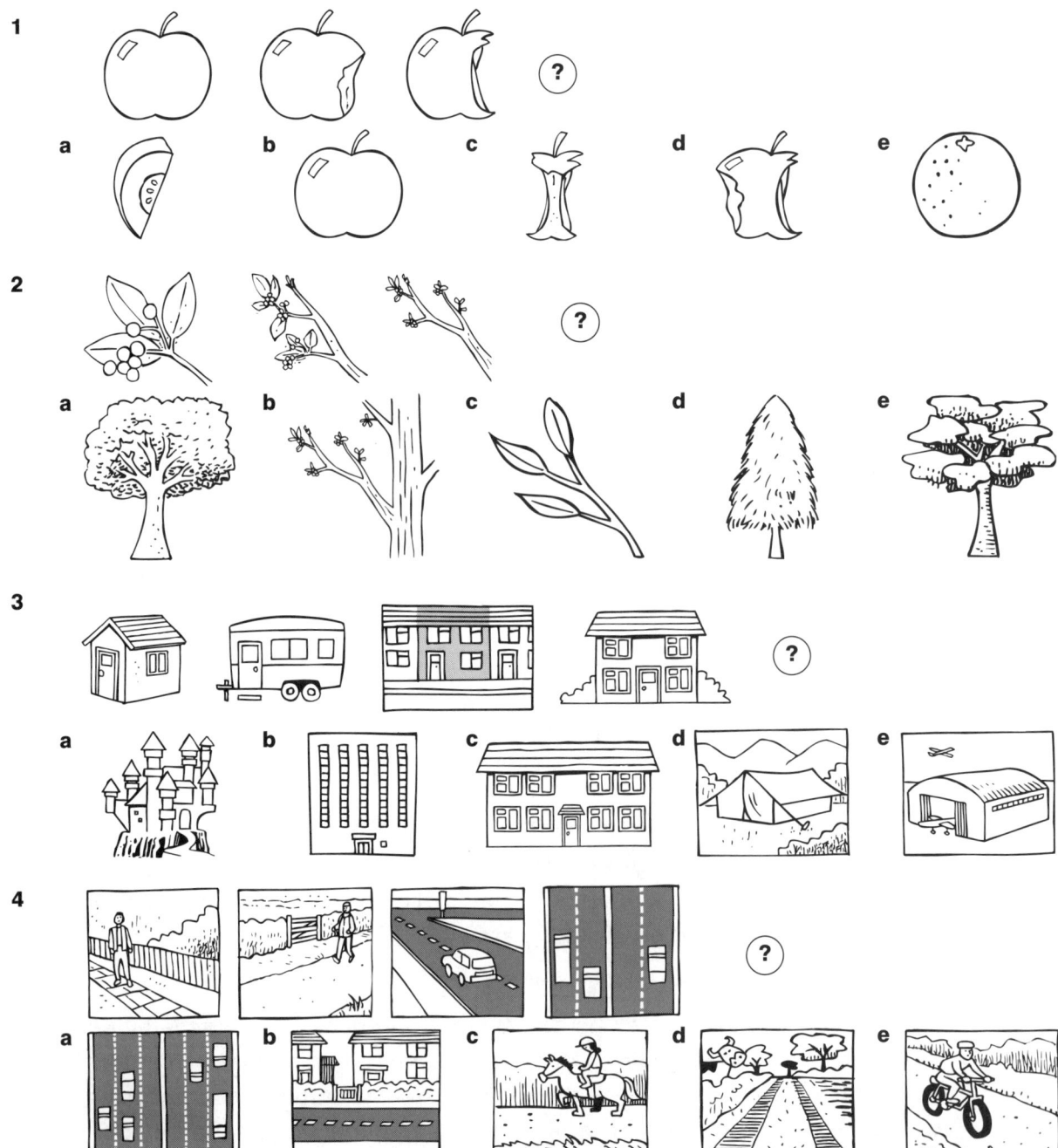

16 | Sequences

Which one comes next?

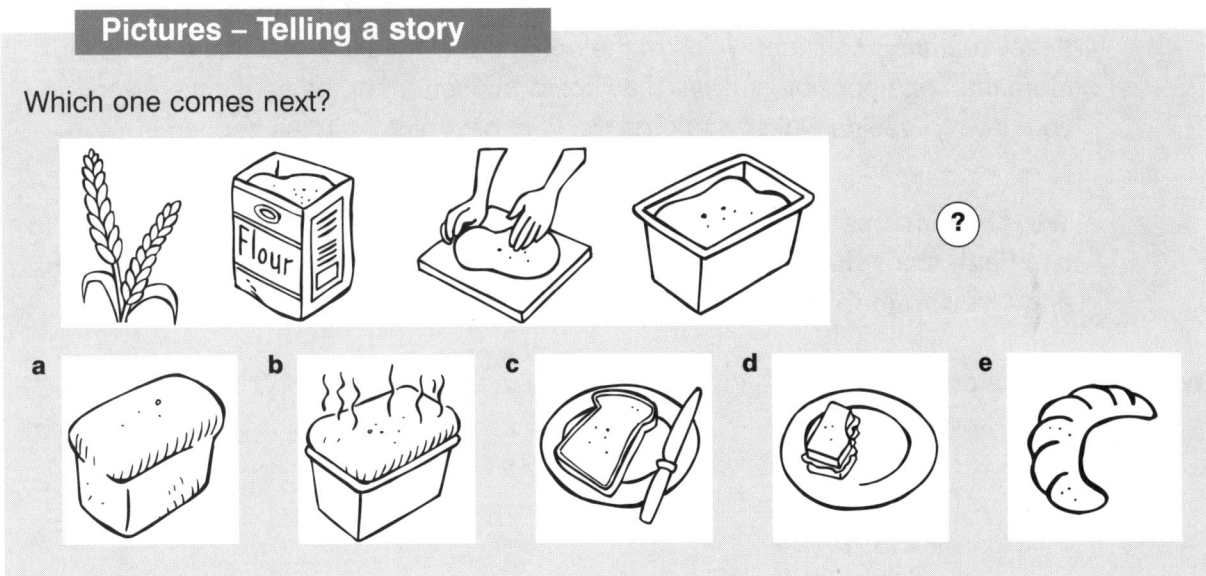

How to do it

Consider: *Repeating pattern — Does the first picture reappear in the pattern?* **No.**

So it is not a repeating pattern.

Shape — is there a regular pattern to the shapes of the objects?
The objects are all different shapes.

There is no regular shape pattern.

Position — are the objects in different positions?

There is no pattern to the positions of the objects.

Angle — is there a pattern to the angles of the pictures?
The pictures are all at different angles.

There is no regular pattern to their angles.

Number — are there any number patterns to the pictures?
There is one ear of wheat, one bag of flour, some dough and two hands, and dough and a tin, but there is no regular pattern to the numbers.

Shading — are the pictures shaded differently?

There is no pattern to the shading of the pictures.

Size — are the pictures different sizes?
There is no pattern to the sizes of the pictures — some are different sizes to others but there is no regular pattern.

33

So what is the sequence?

When you can't see a sequence using **SPANSS**, consider whether the pictures are telling a story. That is, think about if the sequence is a time sequence.

If they are, then consider which of the options provides the next stage in the story. More than one possible answer may seem to occur after the sequence given, so you have to decide which would be the very next picture in the sequence.

Do the pictures tell a story?

Yes, the pictures are different stages in making bread. The wheat grows in the field, then the wheat is made into flour, the flour is made into dough, and the dough is placed in the oven.

Work through the possible answers to find the very next stage in the story.

	what's the story?	*is it after the dough is placed in the oven?*
a	a baked loaf of bread	yes
b	a fresh baked loaf of bread	yes
c	a slice of bread	yes
d	a half-eaten slice of bread	yes
e	a croissant	no — nothing to do with this story

Four of the possible answers come after the ones given in the sequence.

Now work out which is the **very next** stage after placing the dough in the oven.

*Which of the possible answers would come **first**?*

when in the story

a after cooking it, before eating it
b just after cooking it, when it is still hot
c after cooking it and after slicing it up, before eating it
d while you are eating it

Answer a and answer b are very close, but answer b comes first because the loaf is fresh from the oven, still in its baking tin.

So the answer is **b**.

Now try these

Which one comes next?

1

a    b    c    d    e

2

a    b    c    d    e

3

a    b 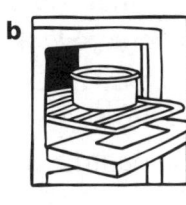   c    d    e

4

a    b 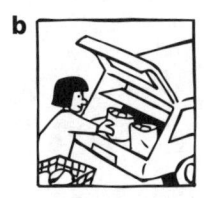   c    d    e

17 Analogies

Which one comes next?

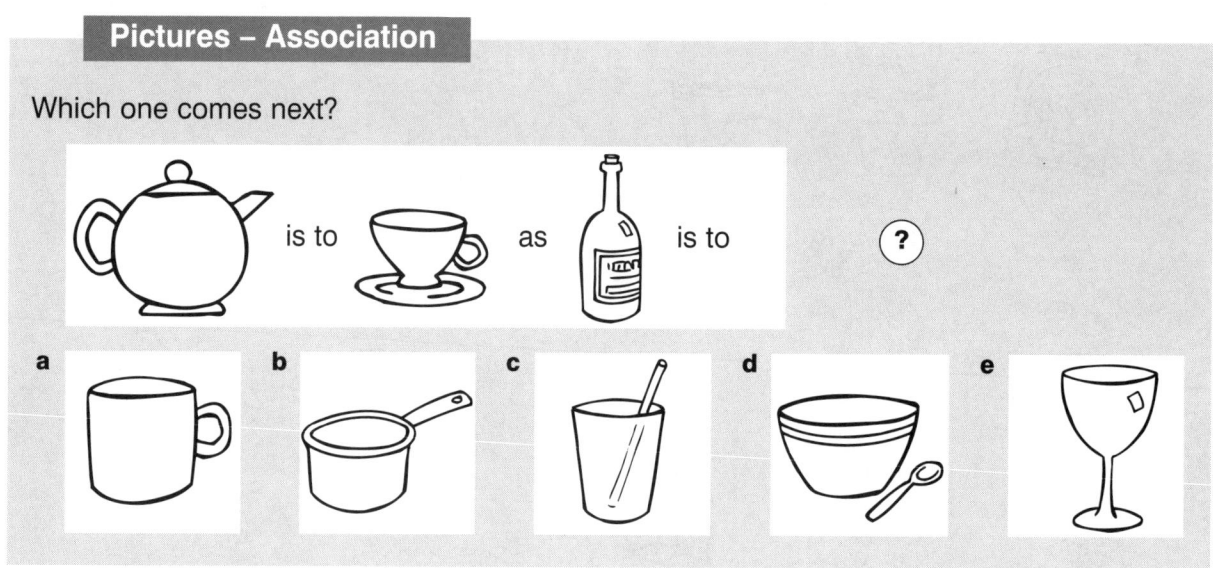

How to do it

To answer these questions you need to consider the relationship or association between the first two pictures and apply it to the second picture.

First pair — what is the relationship?

The first pair is a teapot and a cup and saucer. The teapot contains tea, which is poured into the cup and saucer. You drink the tea from the cup and saucer.

Second pair — what is the equivalent relationship or association?

The first picture in the second pair is a bottle. A bottle contains a cold drink. This bottle looks like it holds wine.

Work through the possible answers, looking for something into which you would pour a cold drink from a bottle. Remember that you are looking for the best answer.

	what is it?	*would you pour wine into it to drink?*
a	a mug	maybe, but not usually
b	a saucepan	you might pour wine into food while cooking, but not to drink
c	a glass with straw	possibly, but not usually
d	a bowl	no
e	a wine glass	yes

The best answer is **e**, the wine glass.

Are there any other associations or relationships between the first two pictures?
No, so the answer is **e**.

Now try these

Choose the picture which completes the second pair in the same way as the first pair.

Symbols – Shape

Which is the odd one out?

a   b   c   d   e

How to do it

Shape — What shapes make up each symbol?

Look at the shape of each one:

a *circle*   **b** *circle*   **c** *circle*   **d** *oval*   **e** *circle*

All of the symbols are circles apart from d, which is an oval.

So **d** is the odd one out.

Now check there are no other variables that could give answers.

Is there an odd one out in terms of:

Position   — **no.**

Angle   — **no.**

Number   — **no.**

Shading   — **no — they are all shaded differently.**

Size   — **no — they are all different sizes.**

So the answer is **d**.

Now try these

Which is the odd one out?

1   a   b   c   d   e

2   a   b   c   d   e

3   a   b   c   d   e

4   a   b   c   d   e

19 Similarities

Which is the odd one out?

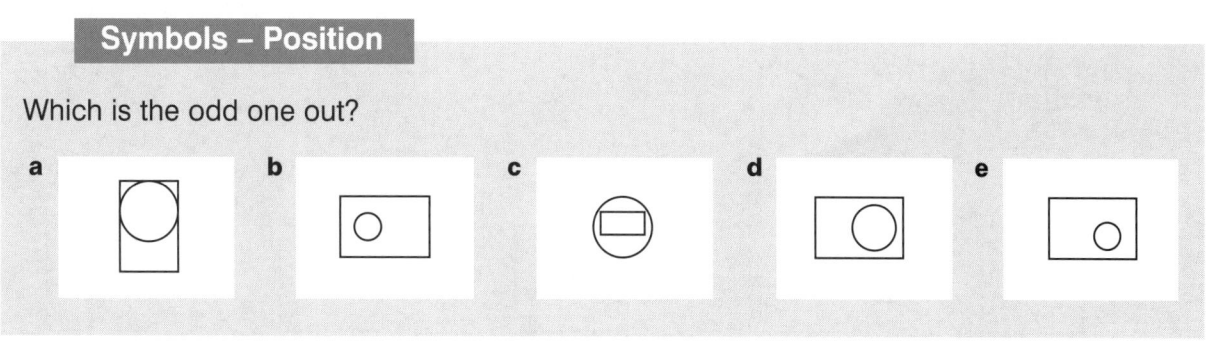

a   b   c   d   e

How to do it

Shape — What shapes make up each symbol?
All the symbols are a circle and a rectangle.

So there is no odd one out.

Position — What are the positions of the circle and the rectangle?
Look at each symbol and the relative positions of the two shapes.

- **a** circle inside a rectangle, at the top, touching the sides
- **b** circle inside a rectangle, in the middle, not touching the sides
- **c** rectangle inside a circle, at the top, not touching the sides
- **d** circle inside a rectangle, at the right, touching the sides
- **e** circle inside a rectangle, at the bottom right, not touching the sides

Is there a common feature?
Yes, the circle is inside the rectangle for most of the symbols.
Is there an odd one out?
Yes, **c** is the odd one out because the rectangle is inside the circle.

Now check there are no other variables that could give answers.

Is there an odd one out in terms of:
Angle   — no, they are all at the same angle.
Number   — no.
Shading   — no.
Size   — no.

So the answer is **c**.

Now try these

Which is the odd one out?

1 **a** 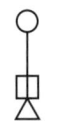 **b**  **c** 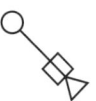 **d** 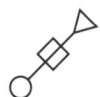 **e**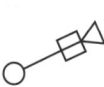

2 **a** 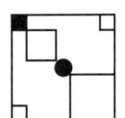 **b** 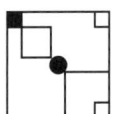 **c** 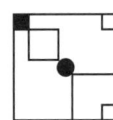 **d** 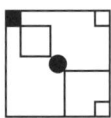 **e**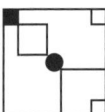

3 **a**  **b**  **c**  **d**  **e**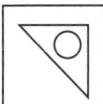

4 **a**  **b**  **c**  **d**  **e**

20 | Similarities

Which is the odd one out?

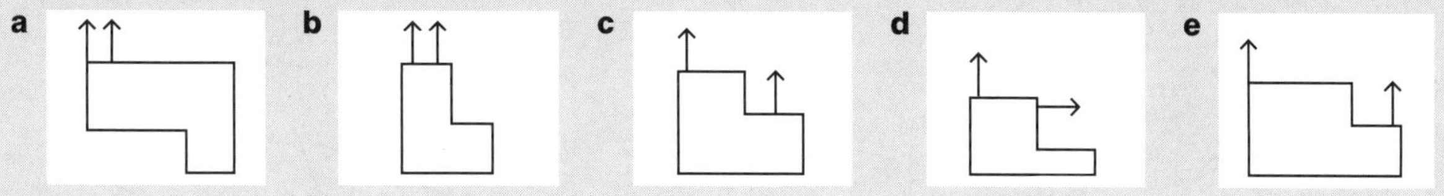

How to do it

Shape — What shape is each object?
Look at the outline shapes.
The outlines are made up of rectangles.
Look at the arrows.
There are two arrows on each shape.

So there is no odd one out.

Position — What is the position of each object?
Look at the outlines and the arrows.
The outlines are in different positions.
The arrows are all in different positions.

Angle — What are the angles of the arrows?
Look at each pair of arrows:

    a *both vertical*   **b** *both vertical*   **c** *both vertical*
    d *one vertical, one horizontal*   **e** *both vertical*

The arrows on d are at right angles to each other.

So **d** is the odd one out.

Now check there are no other variables that could give answers.

Is there an odd one out in terms of:
Number — **no, there are always two arrows.**
Shading — **no.**
Size   — **no.**

So the answer is **d**.

Now try these

Which is the odd one out?

1   **a**    **b**    **c**    **d**    **e**

2   **a**    **b**    **c**    **d**    **e**

3   **a**   **b**   **c** 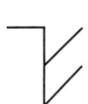   **d**   **e**

4   **a** 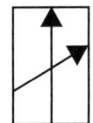   **b**    **c**    **d** 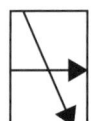   **e**

Symbols – Number

Which is the odd one out?

a 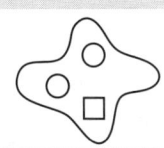   b    c 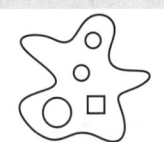   d    e

How to do it

Shape — What shapes are in each object?
The outline shapes are all different.
The inside shapes are circles and squares.

So there is no odd one out.

Position — What is the position of each object?
Look at the shapes inside the outlines.
They are all in different positions.

So there is no odd one out.

Angle — Are the shapes in certain rotational positions?
The shapes are not rotations.

So there is no odd one out.

Number — How many shapes are inside each outline?
Look at the number of circles and squares in each shape.

	how many circles?	*how many squares?*
a	2	1
b	2	1
c	3	1
d	2	1
e	2	1

There are 2 circles and 1 square in each outline apart from **c**,
which has 3 circles and 1 square.

So **c** is the odd one out.

Now check there are no other variables that could give answers.

Is there an odd one out in terms of:

Shading — **no.**

Size — **no.**

So the answer is **c**.

Now try these

Which is the odd one out?

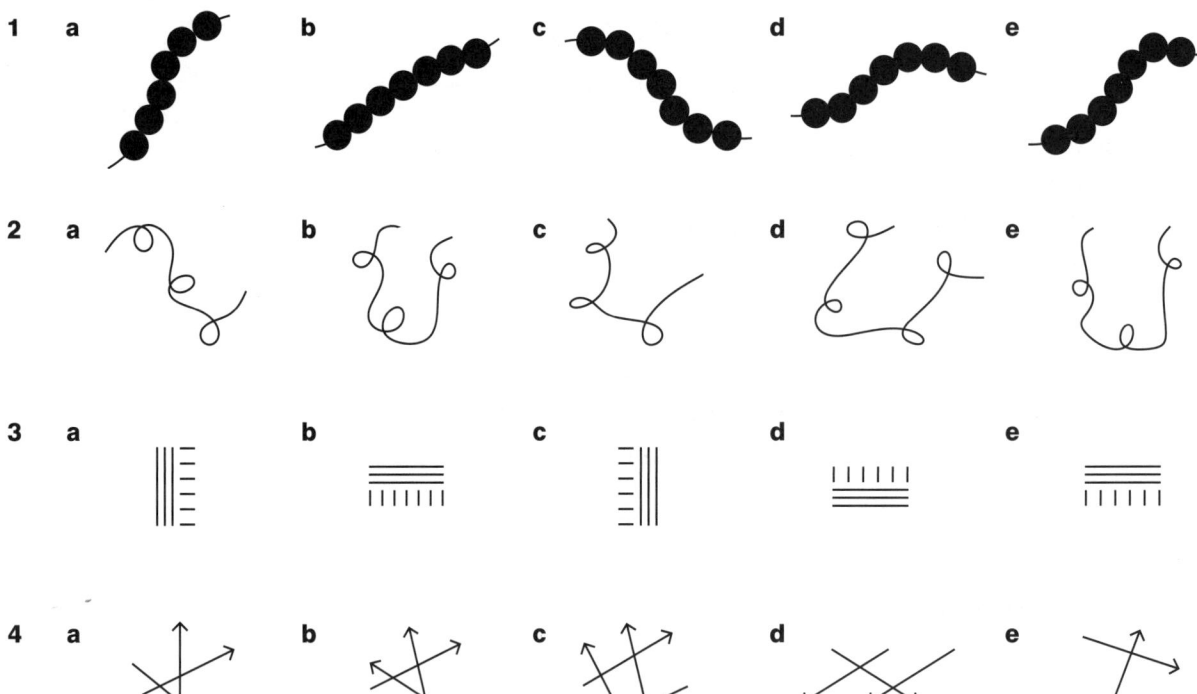

Symbols – Shading

Which is the odd one out?

a 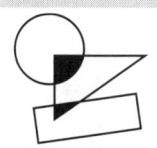 b  c 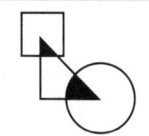 d 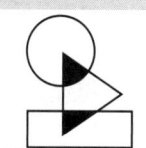 e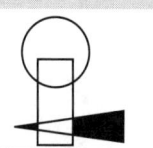

How to do it

Shape — What shape are the objects?

Look at each shape in each symbol.

All the symbols have a circle, a triangle and a rectangle.

So there is no odd one out.

Position — What is the position of each shape?

Look at how the shapes overlap.

They all overlap with one other shape, in different ways.

So there is no odd one out.

Angle — Are the angles of the shapes the same?

Look at how the shapes are arranged.

There is no rotation in the arrangements.

So there is no odd one out.

Shading — Are there any patterns in the shading?

Look at the shaded areas.

All the symbols have shaded areas where the shapes overlap except for e, which does not have its overlapping areas shaded.

So **e** is the odd one out.

Is there an odd one out in terms of:

Size — **no.**

So the answer is **e**.

Now try these

Which is the odd one out?

1   a 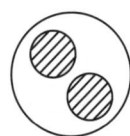   b 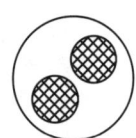   c 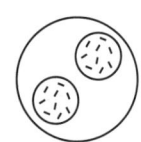   d 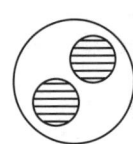   e

2   a    b 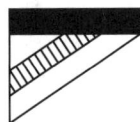   c    d 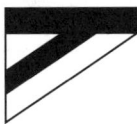   e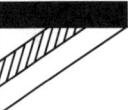

3   a 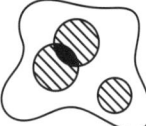   b    c    d 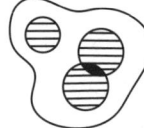   e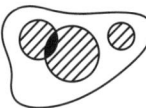

4   a 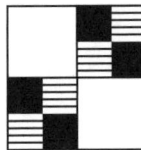   b 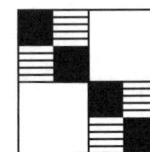   c 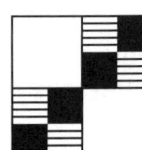   d 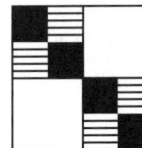   e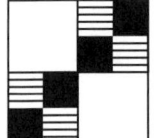

23 Similarities

Which is the odd one out?

How to do it

Shape — What shape is each symbol?
They are all circles.
So there is no odd one out.

Position — What is the position of each symbol?
They are all in the same position.
So there is no odd one out.

Angle — What angles are involved in each circle?
The circles are not divided, so no angles are involved.
So there is no odd one out.

Number — What numbers are involved in each symbol?
They are all single circles.
So there is no odd one out.

Shading — What is the shading of each circle?
The circles are all shaded differently apart from b and d, which are the same.
So there is no odd one out.

Size — What is the size of each circle?
The circles are all the same size apart from d, which is smaller.
So **d** is the odd one out.

There are no other variables to check.
So the answer is **d**.

Now try these

Which is the odd one out?

1 a   b   c   d   e

2 a   b   c   d   e

3 a   b   c   d   e

4 a   b   c   d   e

Symbols – More than one variable

Shape and Number
Which pattern on the right belongs in the group on the left?

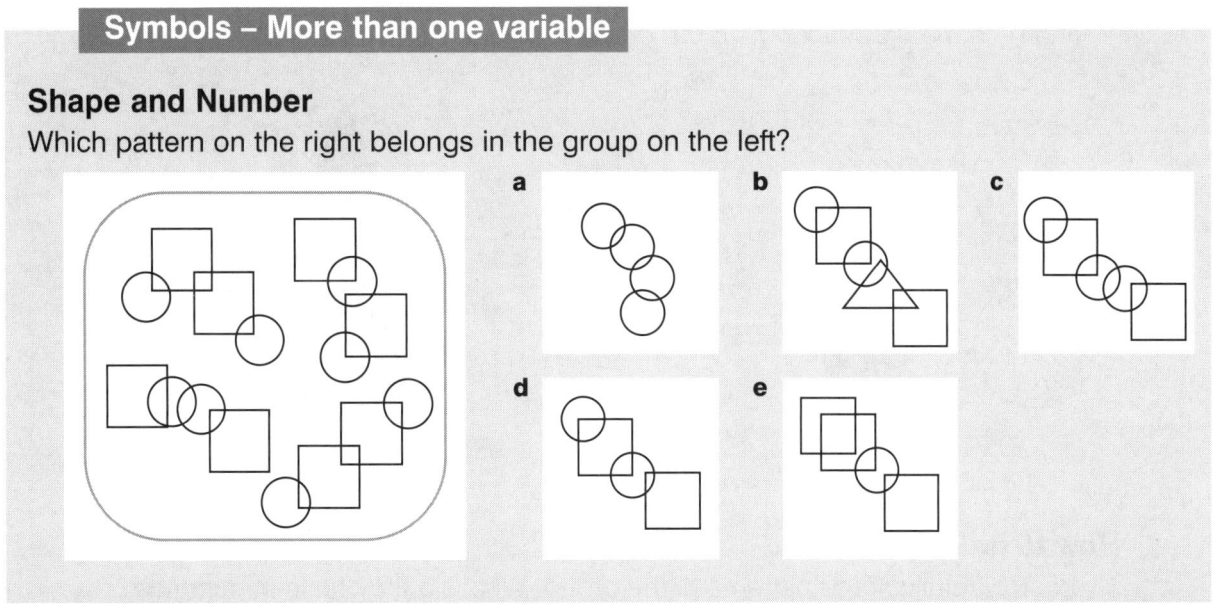

How to do it

This type of question often means there are two variables in common to the group on the left. Look carefully at the patterns in the group. What do they have in common?

Shape	— **yes, they are all circles and rectangles.**
Position	— **no, they are all in different positions.**
Angle	— **no, they are all at different angles.**
Number	— **yes, each symbol has two rectangles and two circles.**
Shading	— **there is no shading.**
Size	— **they are all the same size.**

It is very important to check all the categories as there can be more than one or two common features.

When you have worked out the common features (in this case, there are 2 circles and 2 rectangles in each symbol in the group), work through each of the possible answers in turn.

	2 circles?	*2 rectangles?*
a	no, 4	no, 0
b	yes	yes, but also a triangle
c	no, 3	yes
d	yes	yes
e	no, 1	no, 3

So the answer is **d**.

Sometimes it might seem that there is more than one answer. If so, look again at the symbols in the circle and try to find another variable or common feature, such as size or shading.

Shape, Position and Shading

Which pattern on the right belongs in the group on the left?

a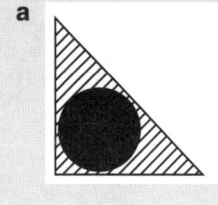
b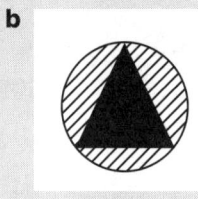
c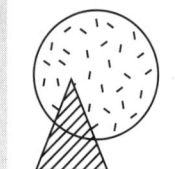
d
e

How to do it

Look carefully at the patterns in the group. What do they have in common?

Shape — yes, they all have a triangle and a circle.

Position — yes, they all have the triangle inside the circle.

Angle — no, there are various angles.

Number — yes, there is 1 circle and 1 triangle in each symbol.

Shading — yes, the triangle is always filled with lines.

Size — no, they are of different sizes.

Now look at the possible answers to see what features are relevant. If all the possible answers have a feature in common, that feature won't help us find the answer.

Are all the answers a triangle and a circle?

No, d is 2 circles.

So we can exclude answer **d**.

Are all the answers a triangle inside a circle?

No, a is a circle inside a triangle, and c is a triangle overlapping a circle.

So we can exclude **a** and **c**.

We have narrowed down the possible answers to **b** and **e**.

*Does **b** or **e** have a triangle shaded with lines?*

Yes, e has a triangle shaded with lines, b has a triangle shaded black.

So the answer is **e**.

Now check with your list of common features.

*Shape and Number — Does **e** have a triangle and a circle?* **Yes.**

Position — Is the triangle inside the circle? **Yes.**

Shading — Is the triangle shaded with lines? **Yes.**

So the answer must be **e**.

Angle and size

Which pattern on the right belongs in the group on the left?

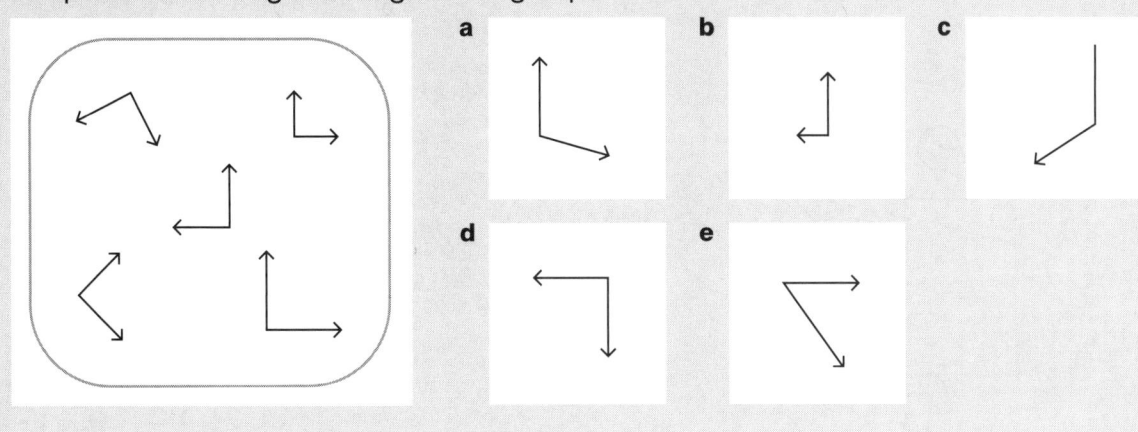

Look carefully at the symbols in the group. What do they have in common?

Shape — yes, the shapes are all arrows.

Position — no, they are all in different positions.

Angle — yes, they are all at right angles.

Number — yes, there are two lines in each symbol.

Shading — no, there is no shading.

Size — yes, both lines are the same length as each other in a pair.

Now look at the possible answers to see what features are relevant. If all the possible answers have a feature in common, that feature will not help us find the answer.

Are all the possible answers arrows?
Yes, so that will not help us to narrow down the answers.

Are all the possible answers at right angles?
No, a, c and e are not at right angles, so we can discard those answers.

Are there two lines in each of the possible answers?
Yes, so that will not help us to narrow down the answers.

*Are both of the possible answers, **b** and **d**, pairs of lines of equal length?*
No, b has arrows of differing lengths.

So the answer must be d.

Now check with your list of common features.

Shape and Number — is **d** made up of 2 arrows?   **Yes.**

Angle — is **d** two arrows at right angles?   **Yes.**

Size — are the two arrows in **d** the same length as each other?   **Yes.**

So the answer must be d.

Now try these

These questions have different variables in common.
Which pattern on the right belongs in the group on the left?

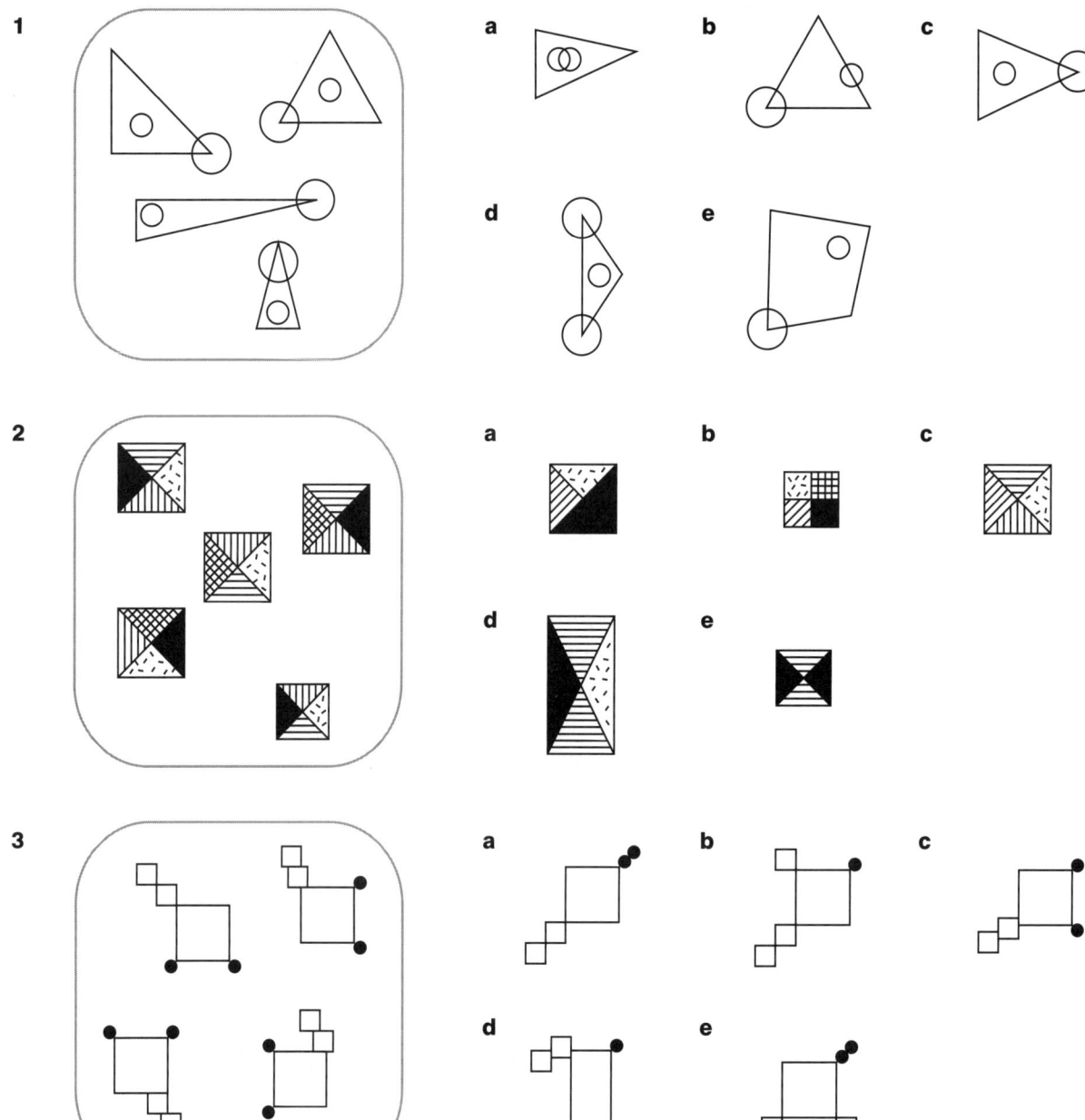

1

a   b   c

d   e

2

a   b   c

d   e

3

a   b   c

d   e

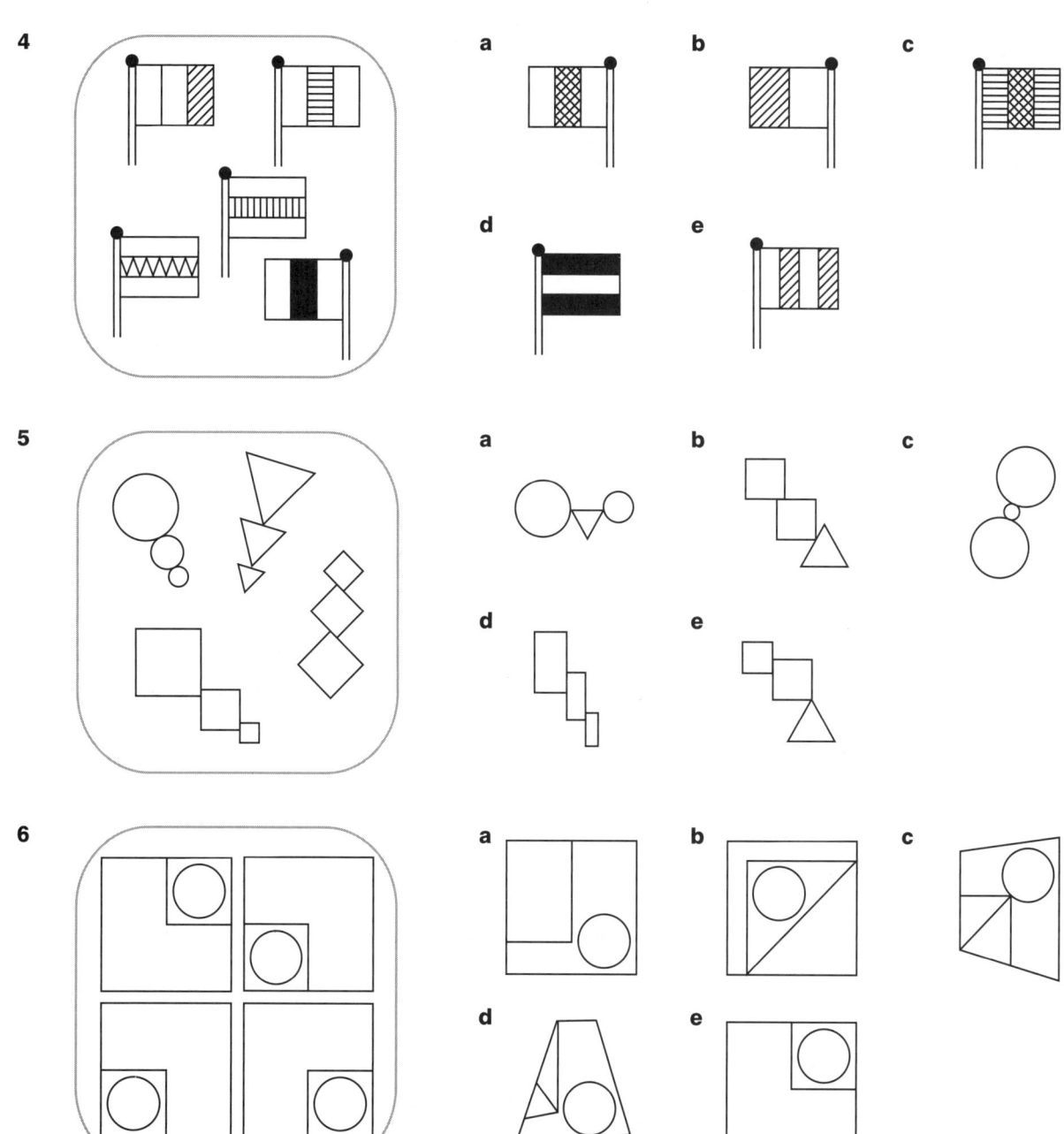

Symbols – Repeating Patterns

Which one comes next?

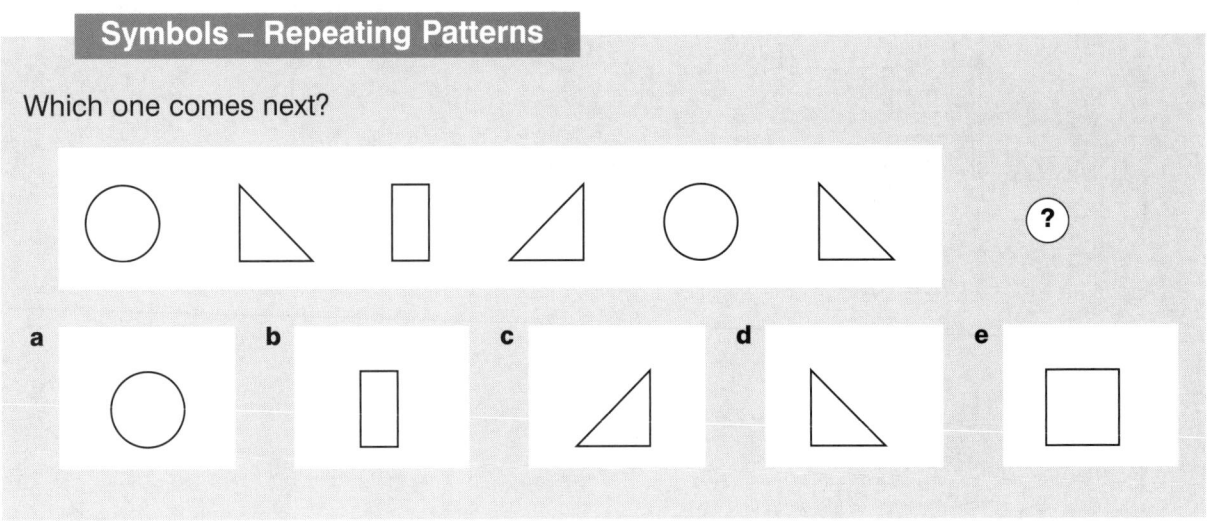

How to do it

Look carefully at the patterns in the sequence. Is the first one repeated?

If so, underline the repeating section — from the first shape to just before that shape is repeated.

This makes up the repeating block.

Now match the shapes one by one until you find out which of the possible answers should come next.

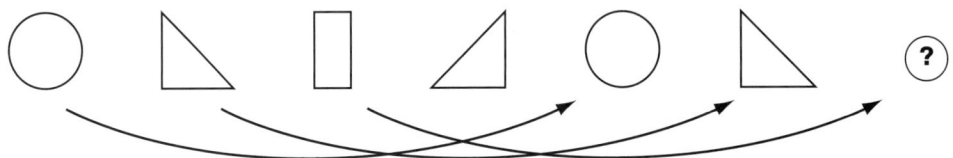

In this example, the answer would be the rectangle, answer **b**.

Now try these

Which one comes next?

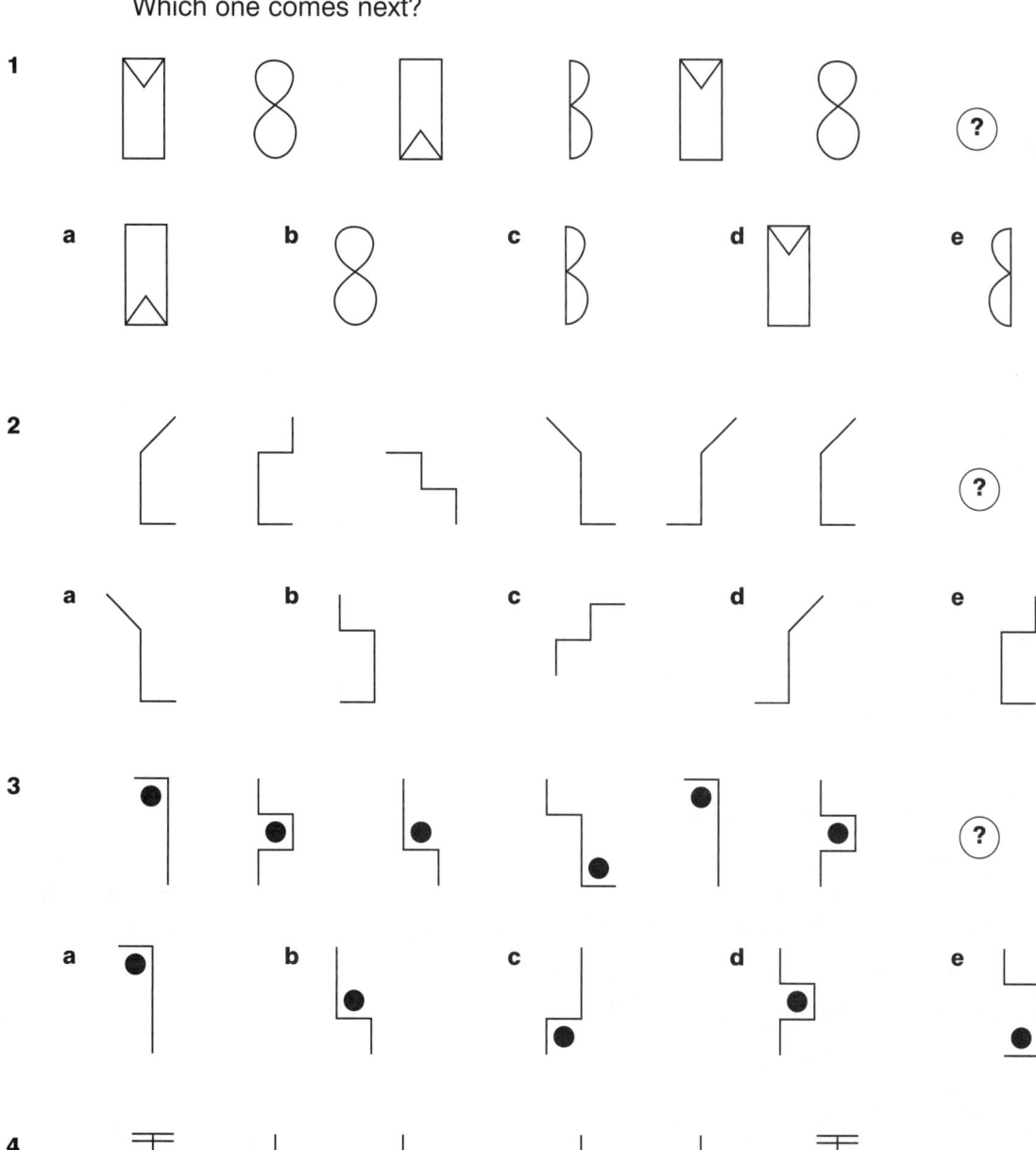

26 Sequences

Which one comes next?

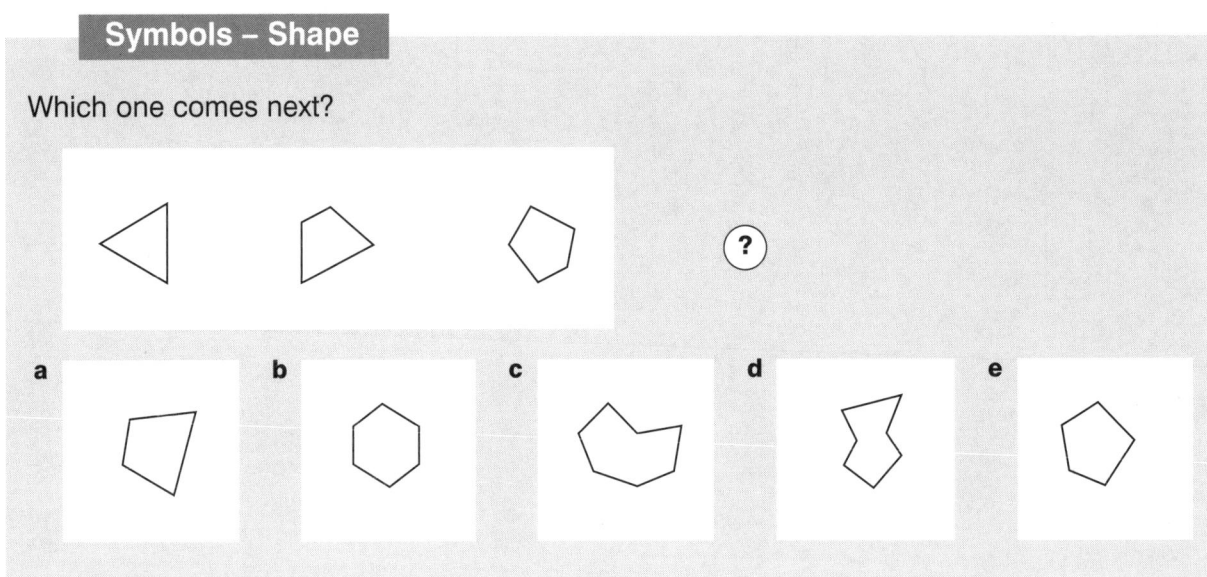

How to do it

Repeating pattern — is the first shape repeated along the line?
No, so it is not a repeating pattern.

Shape — Do the shapes change in a regular way?
Look at the shapes and how they change.
The first shape has 3 sides, the second shape has 4 sides and the third shape has 5 sides. There is one more side each time. This means that the next shape in the sequence must have 6 sides — it must be a hexagon.
Work through the possible answers looking for a hexagon.
Answer b is the only hexagon.

So the answer is **b**.

Is there a regular sequence in terms of:
Position — **no.**
Angle — **no.**
Number — **yes, but only the number of sides.**
Shading — **no.**
Size — **no.**

Now try these

Which one comes next?

1

   ?

a  b c  d e

2

 ?

a b c  d e

3

  ?

a  b 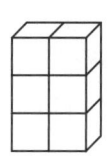 c 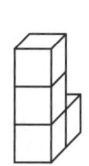 d 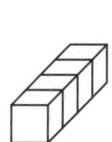 e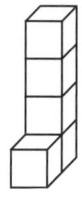

4

 ?

a  b  c  d  e

27 | Sequences

Symbols – Position

Which one comes next?

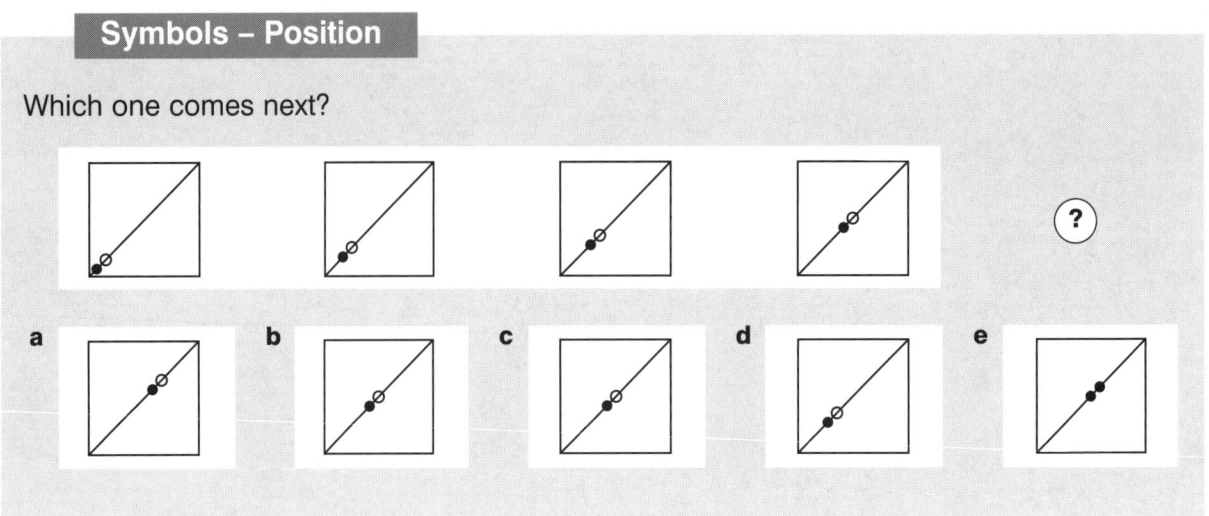

How to do it

Repeating pattern — is the first shape repeated along the line?
No, so it is not a repeating pattern.

Shape — do the shapes change in a regular way?
All the symbols have a box, a line and two circles.
So there is no sequence of shape.

Position — does the position of any of the symbols change?
The two circles move together along the diagonal line towards the top right-hand corner of the box as the sequence progresses.
From the changing positions of the circles you now need to predict the next symbol in the sequence.

prediction

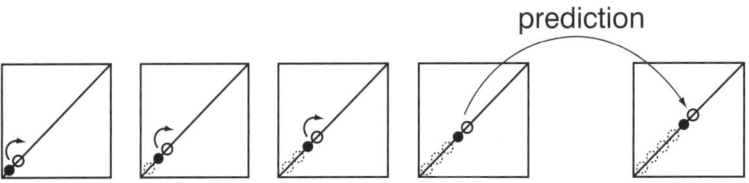

Now work through the possible answers to find the matching symbol.

	further along the line?	are the circles together?
a	yes	yes
b	no	yes
c	no	no
d	no	yes
e	yes	yes

So there are two possible answers from looking at the position of the shapes.

Now check for any other variable features.

Angle — *do the shapes rotate or change angle?* **No.**

Number — *does the number of shapes change?* **No.**

Shading — *does the shading of shapes change?* **No, it stays the same.**

This means that the answer must also have the same shading.
Answer a matches the shading, but answer e has two shaded circles,
not one white circle and one shaded circle.

So the answer must be **a**.

Size — does the size of any of the shapes change? **No.**

So the answer is **a**.

Now try these

Which one comes next?

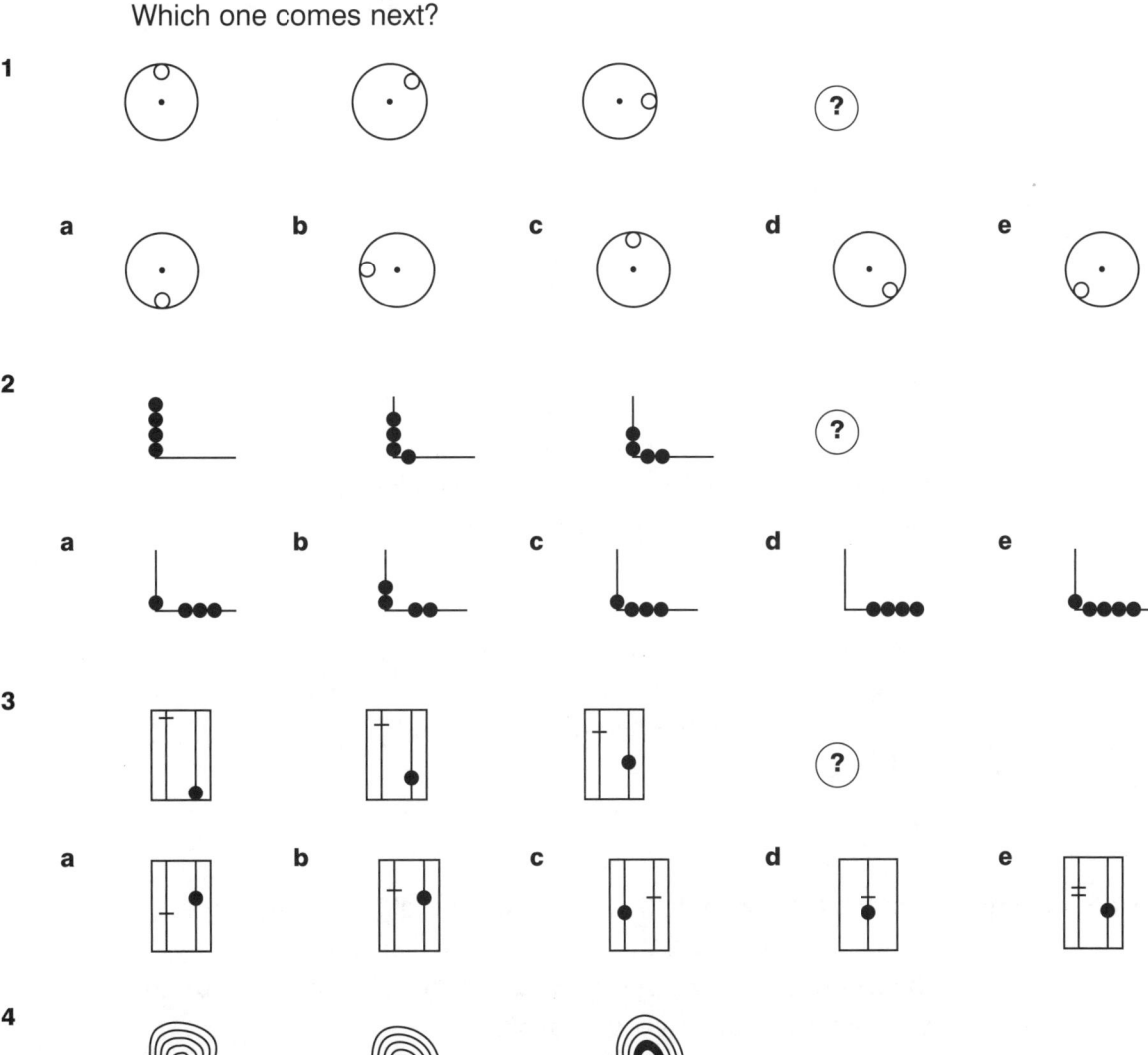

59

Symbols – Angle

Which one comes next?

a   **b**   **c**   **d**   **e**

How to do it

Repeating pattern — is the first shape repeated along the line?   **No.**
So it is not a repeating pattern.

Shape — is there a sequence, order or pattern to the shapes?
No, each shape is a hexagon.

Position — does the position of the shapes change?
No, but the patterns on the shape change.

Angle — do the patterns rotate as the sequence progresses?
Yes, the shaded and dotted sections move clockwise,
as if the hexagon were rotating by 60° each time.

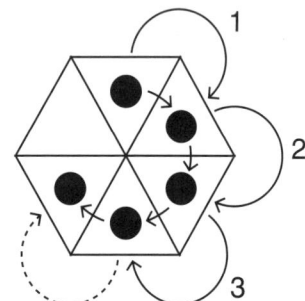

Now you can predict
the next symbol
in the sequence.

Now work through the possible answers to find the next symbol in the sequence.

is each section rotated 60° or one section clockwise?

a   **no, the shaded section is rotated but the dotted section is not**
b   **no, rotated anticlockwise one section**
c   **no, rotated two sections clockwise**
d   **no, rotated two sections anticlockwise**
e   **yes**

So **e** is the answer.

Now check for any other variable features.

Number — *does the number of shapes change?* **No.**

Shading — *does the shading of shapes change?* **Yes, it rotates. You could also say that the shading pattern for each section moves through a repeating pattern like this:**

dotted, white, white, shaded, white, white, dotted.

You only know this, though, by spotting the rotation, because the first shape does not reappear in the sequence as given.

Size — *does the size of any of the shapes change?* **No.**

So the answer is **e**.

Now try these

Which one comes next?

1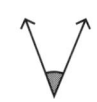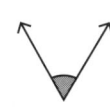

a 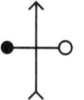 b  c  d 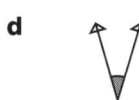 e

2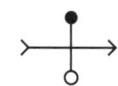

a 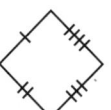 b  c 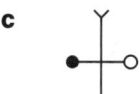 d 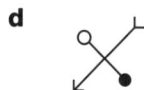 e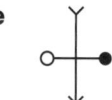

3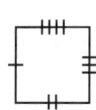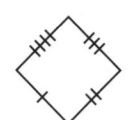

a 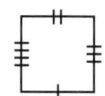 b 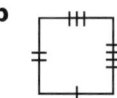 c 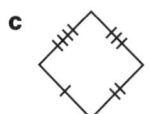 d  e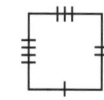

4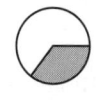

a   b c d e

Symbols – Number

Which one comes next?

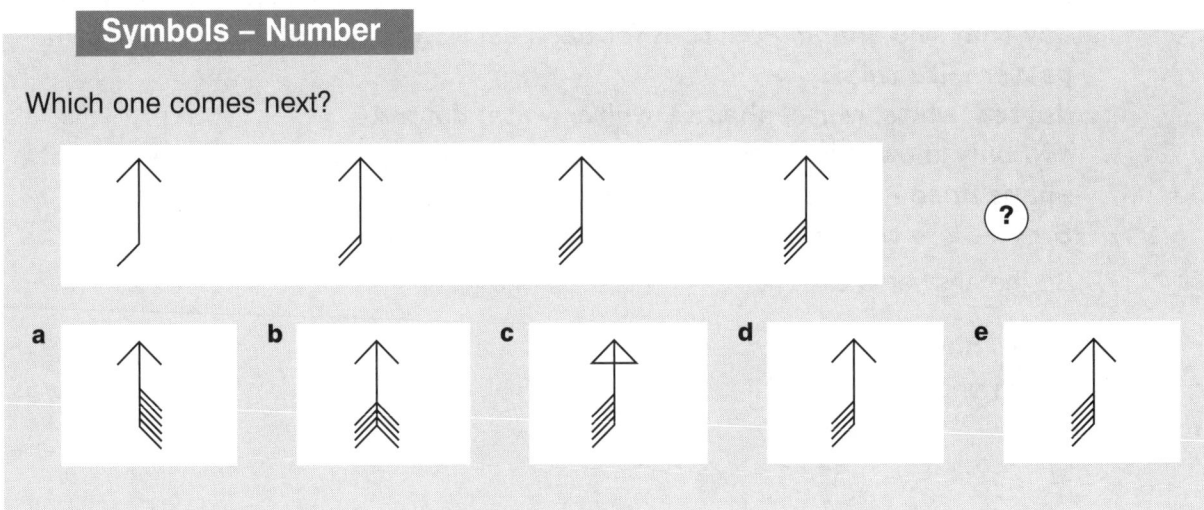

How to do it

Repeating pattern — is the first shape repeated along the line?
No, so it is not a repeating pattern.

Shape — is there a sequence in the shapes?
No, the shapes are all arrows with the same style head.

The arrows have a different number of lines, though — so remember to check the Number.

Position — do the shapes change position?
No, the lines are always on the same side of the arrow.

Angle — is there any change of angle? **No, the arrows are all vertical.**

Number — does the number of parts change?
There is one extra line each time at the bottom of the arrow.

Now you can predict
what the next symbol
will be.

Now work through the possible answers.

	is the head the same?	are the lines on the same side?	are there 5 oblique lines?
a	yes	no	yes
b	yes	no — both sides	no, there are 8
c	no	yes	yes
d	yes	yes	no, there are 4
e	yes	yes	yes

So the answer should be **e**.

Now check for any other variable features.

Shading — does the shading of shapes change?   **No, there is no shading.**

Size — does the size of any of the shapes change?   **No, so the answer should be the same size as the other shapes in the sequence.**

Answer **e** is the same size as the rest of the shapes in the sequence, so **e** is the correct answer.

Now try these

Which one comes next?

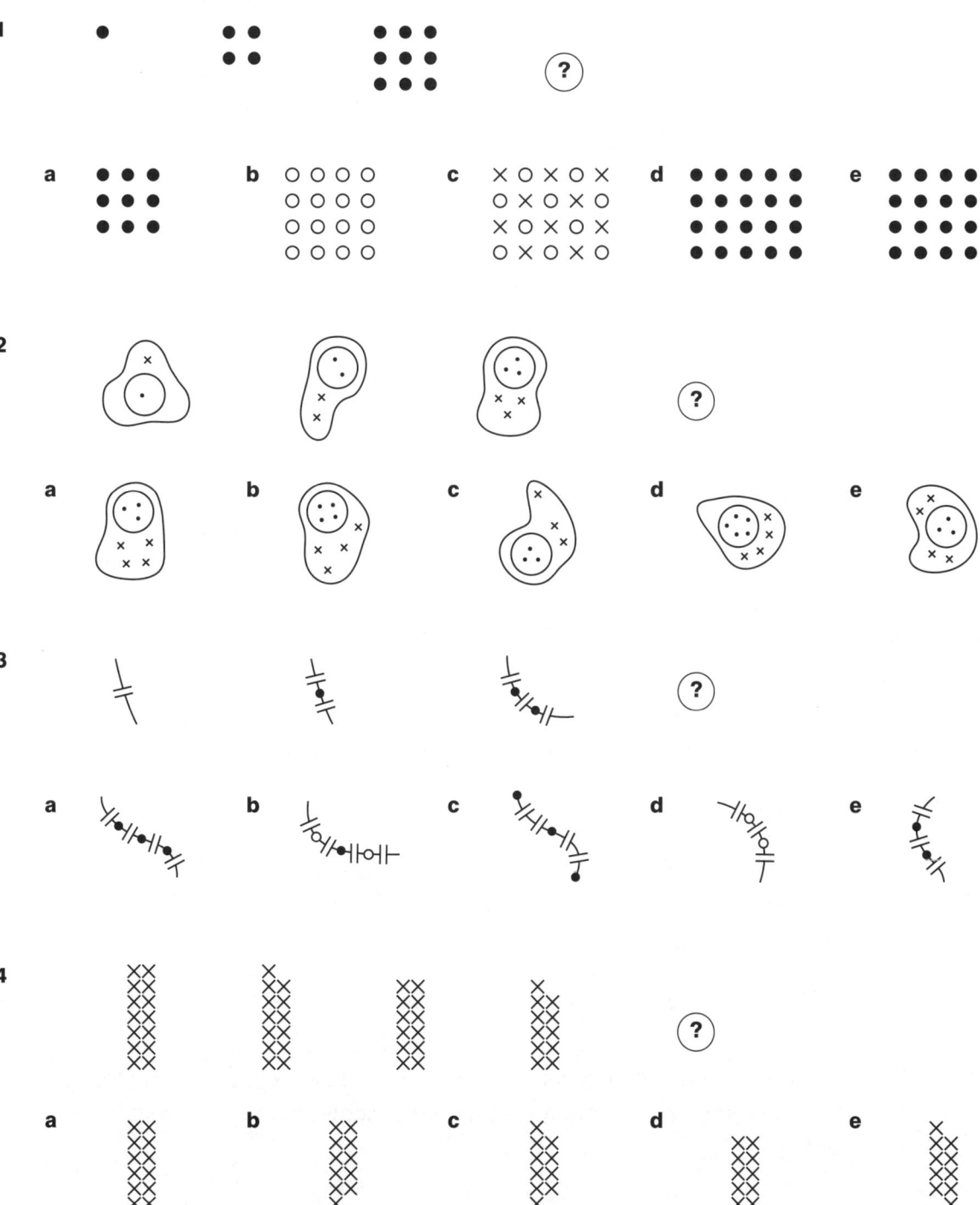

63

Symbols – Shading

Which one comes next?

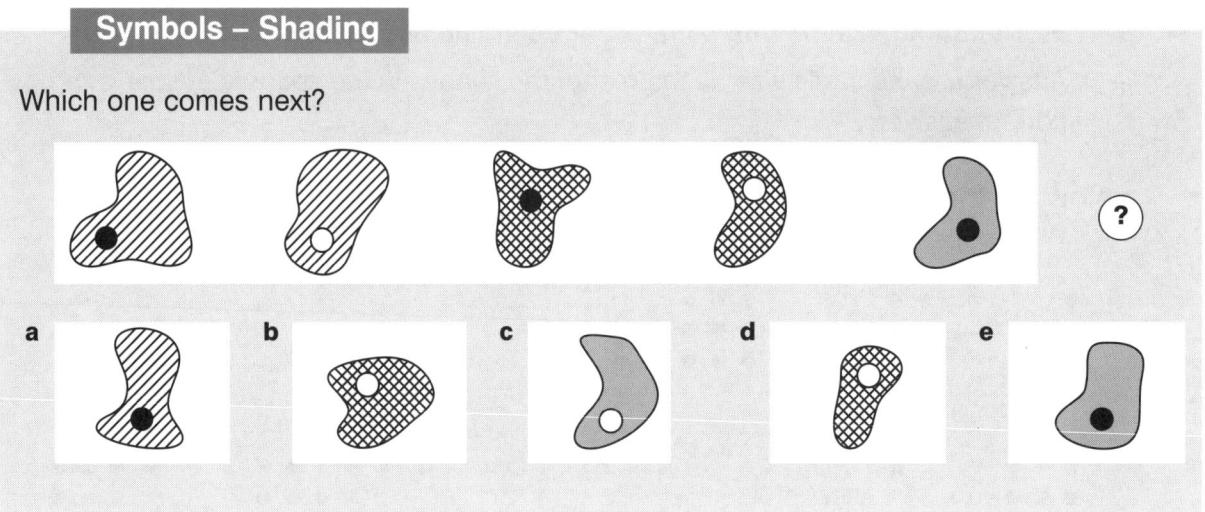

How to do it

Repeating pattern — is the first shape repeated along the line?
No, so it is not a repeating pattern.

Shape — is there a sequence in the shapes?
The outside shapes are all different. They all have a circle in the middle.

Position — do the shapes change position?
No, the circle is always inside the shaded shape.

Angle — *is there any change of angle?* **No, there is no rotation or angle.**
Number — *does the number of parts change?* **No, there is always one circle.**
Shading — *does the shading change?*
Yes, the first two shapes are filled with lines, and the next two shapes are hatched, and the next shape is grey. The circle changes from black to white to black to white to black.

Now you can predict what comes next in the sequence.

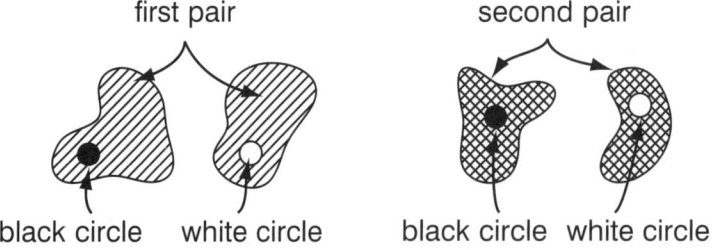

first pair   second pair

black circle   white circle   black circle   white circle

The sequence changes in two ways. One way is in pairs (lines, lines, hatched, hatched and so on) and the other is in a normal sequence (black, white, black, white and so on).

Now work through the possible answers to find the next shape in the sequence.
We are looking for a grey shape with one white circle inside.

	grey shape?	white circle inside?
a	no	no
b	no	yes
c	yes	yes
d	no	yes
e	yes	no

third pair

black circle   white circle

So the answer must be **c**.

Check for any other variables.
Size — does the size change?
The sizes are different, but there is no sequence to the changes.
So the answer is **c**.

Now try these

Which one comes next?

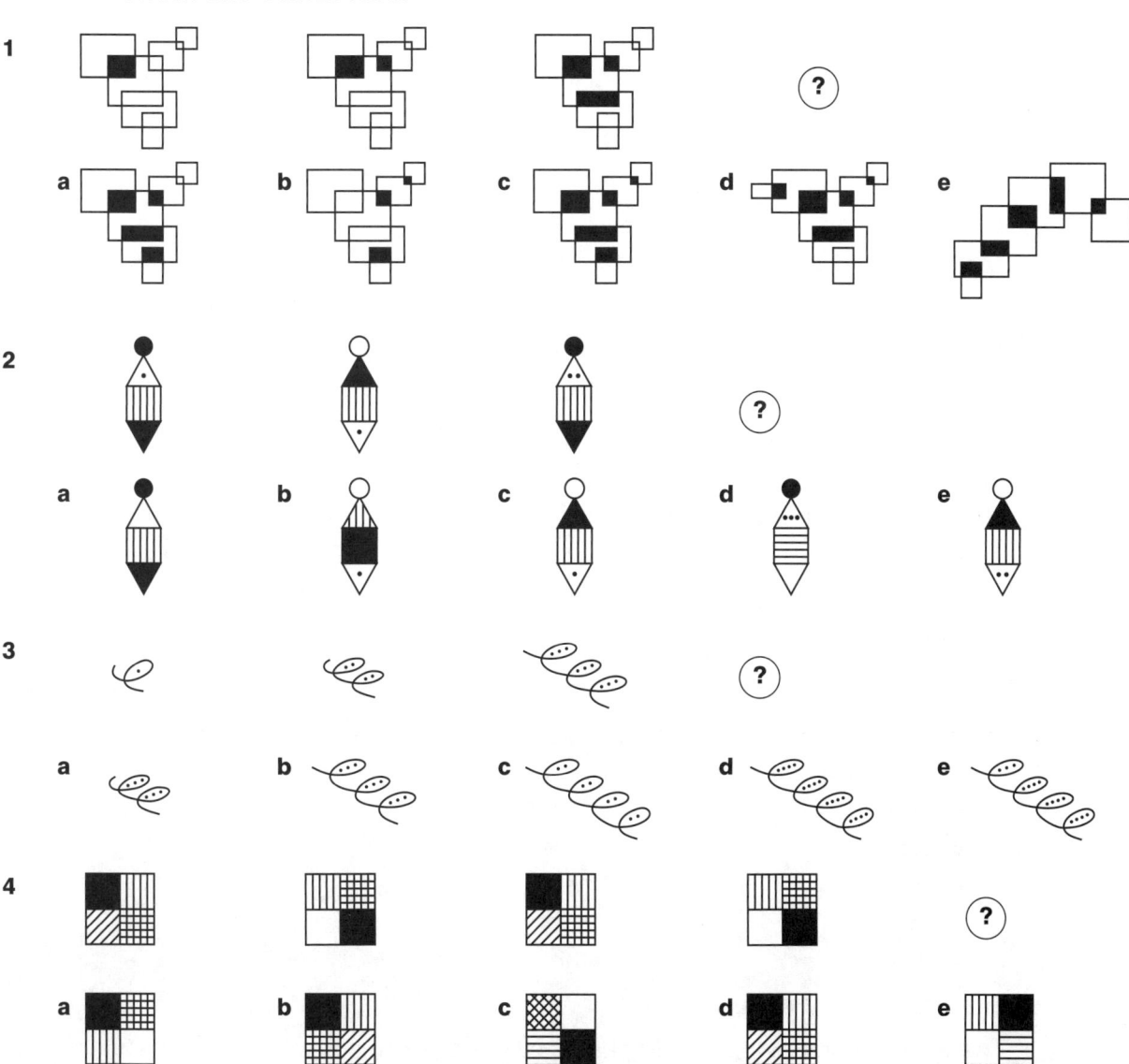

65

Symbols – Size

Which one comes next?

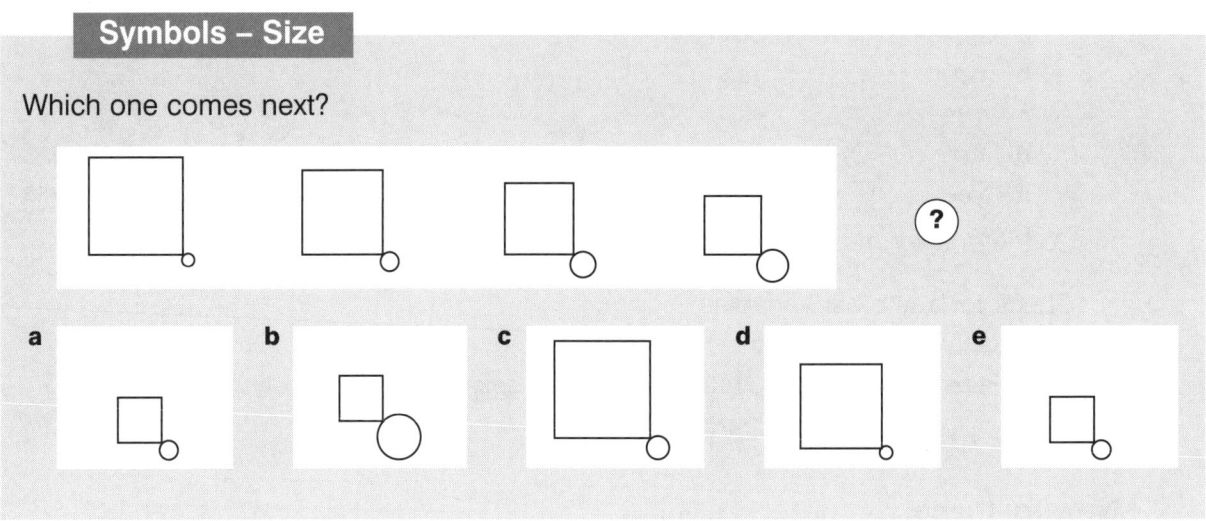

How to do it

Repeating pattern — is the first shape repeated along the line?
No, so it is not a repeating pattern.

Shape — is there a sequence in the shapes?
There is always a square and a circle, but they change size.

Position — do the shapes change position?
No, the circle is always at the corner of the square.

Angle — is there any change of angle? **No, there is no rotation or angle.**

Number — does the number of parts change?
No, there is always one circle and one square.

Shading — does the shading change? **No, there is no shading.**

Size — do the shapes change size?
Yes, the square is getting smaller and the circle is getting bigger.

Now you can predict
the next symbol in the sequence.

Now work through the possible answers to find the next symbol in the sequence.

	is the square smaller?	is the circle bigger?
a	yes	no
b	yes	yes
c	no	no
d	no	no
e	no	no

The answer must be **b**.

There are no more variables to check, so the answer is **b**.

66

Now try these

Which one comes next?

1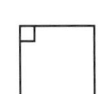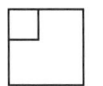

a   **b**   **c**   **d**    **e**

2

a    **b**   **c**    **d**   **e**

3

a    **b**    **c** 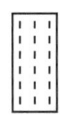   **d**   **e**

4

a 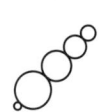   **b**    **c**    **d** 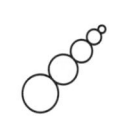   **e**

Analogies

Symbols – Shape

Which pattern on the right completes the second pair in the same way as the first pair?

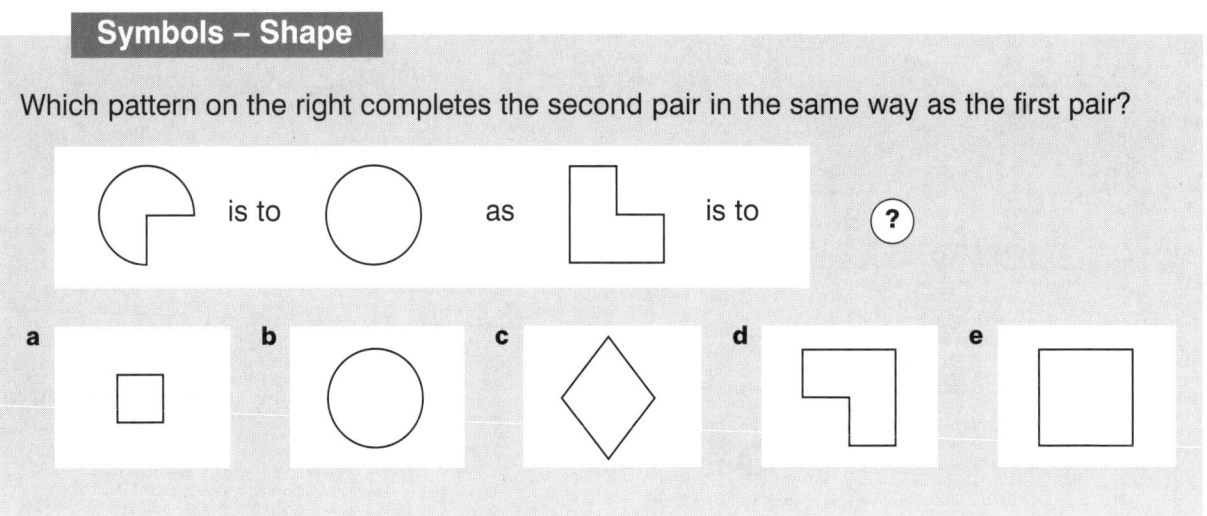

How to do it

Look carefully at the first pair and consider their relationship to each other.

Shape — is there a relationship based on the shapes in the pair?

Yes, the first pattern has a quarter cut away and the second pattern is the complete shape.

Position — The position of the shape has not changed.

Angle — There has not been any rotation of the shape.

Number — There is no change in the number of parts or shapes.

Shading — There is no change of shading in the shapes.

Size — There is no change of size.

Now you can predict the shape that completes the second pair.

The second shape must complete the missing quarter and give the full shape.

Consider each option in turn:

a **is just the missing portion – does not complete the whole shape.**

b **wrong shape**

c **wrong shape**

d **incomplete square**

e **full square – complete shape – is the correct answer.**

So the answer is **e**.

With questions where shape is the key feature, other things like **P**osition, **A**ngle, **N**umber, **S**hading and **S**ize may be included as secondary factors. The important thing is to be quite clear in your mind how the first shape or pattern is related to the second. It often helps to explain the connection in words, then you can apply the same connection to complete the second pair.

Now try these

Which pattern on the right completes the second pair in the same way as the first pair?

1  is to as is to

   a    **b**   **c**   **d**   **e**

2  is to  as  is to

   a    **b**    **c**    **d**    **e**

3  is to  as  is to

   a 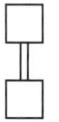   **b**    **c**    **d**    **e**

4 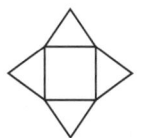 is to  as 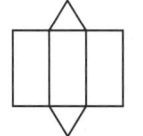 is to

   a    **b**    **c** 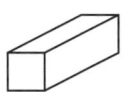   **d** 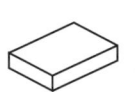   **e**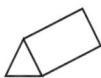

Pictures – Location

Which pattern on the right completes the second pair in the same way as the first pair?

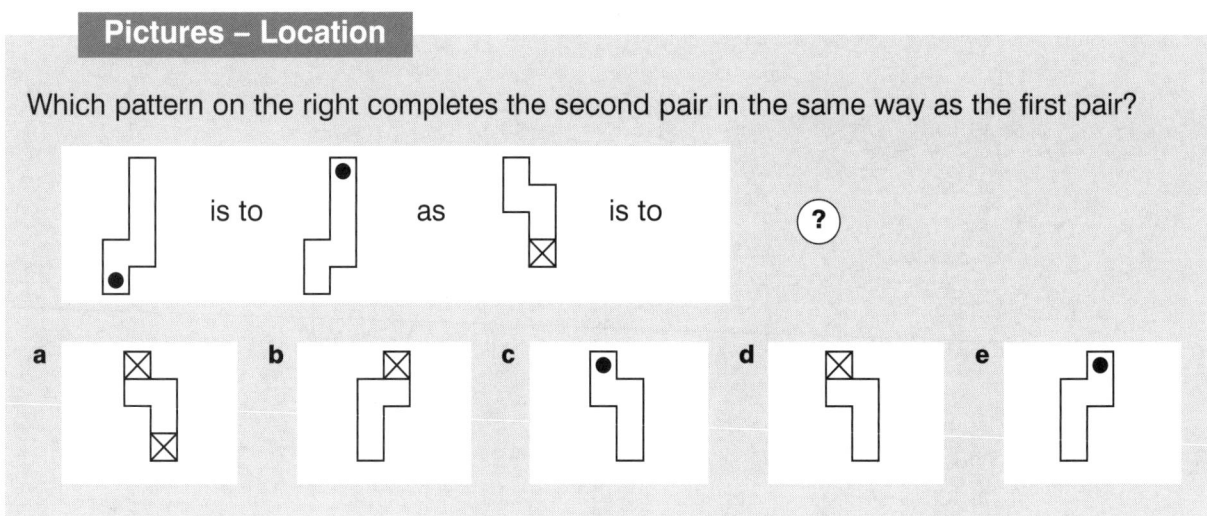

How to do it

Look carefully at the first pair and consider their relationship to each other.

Shape — both are the same shape, and both contain a circle.

Position — the position of the circle has changed from the bottom of the shape to the top of the shape.
The shape itself has stayed in the same position.

Angle — there has not been any change of angle.

Number — there has not been any change of number.

Shading — there is no change of shading.

Size — there is no change of size.

Now you can predict the second shape in the second pair.

The cross in the square is at the bottom, so in the second shape it should be at the top. The shape should not change in any other way.

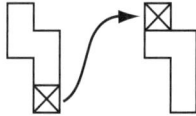

Now work through the answers to find which one completes the second pair.

	same shape?	*cross at the top?*
a	yes	yes, but there's a cross at the bottom as well
b	no	yes
c	yes	no
d	yes	yes
e	no	no

So the answer is **d**.

Now try these

Which pattern on the right completes the second pair in the same way as the first pair?

1 is to as  is to

a    **b**    **c**   **d**   **e**

2 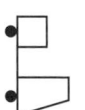 is to 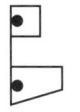 as  is to

a    **b**    **c**    **d**    **e**

3 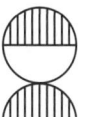 is to 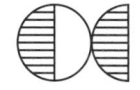 as  is to

a 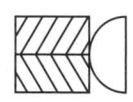   **b**    **c** 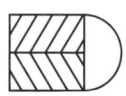   **d** 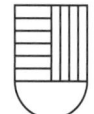   **e**

4 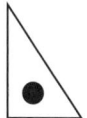 is to 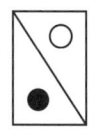 as is to

a   **b**   **c** 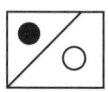   **d** 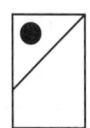   **e**

34 Analogies

Which pattern on the right completes the second pair in the same way as the first pair?

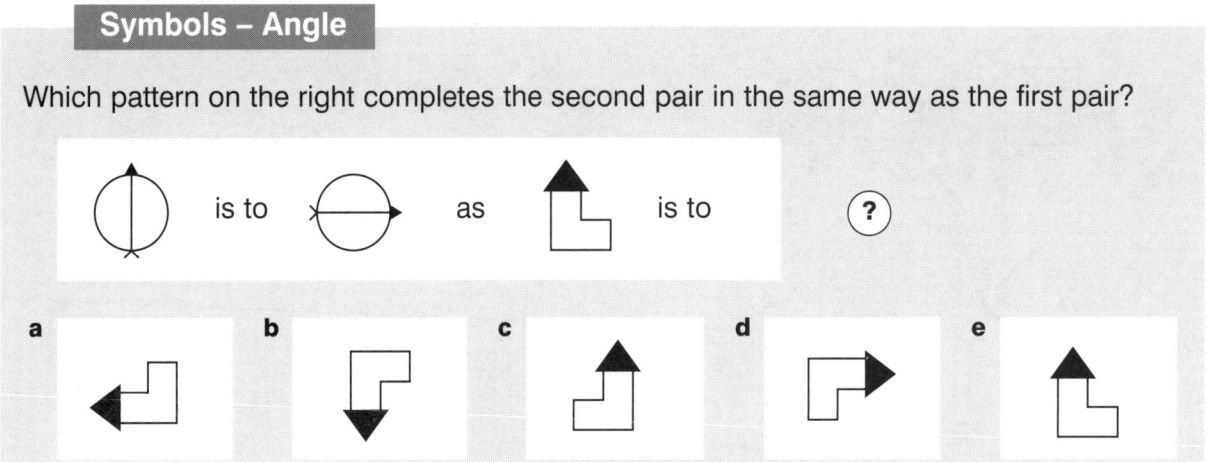

How to do it

Look carefully at the first pair of shapes and consider their relationship to each other.

Shape — the shape itself has not changed.

Position — the position has changed — it has rotated.

Angle — the second shape has been turned clockwise 90° (through a right angle).

Number — the number of shapes has not changed.

Shading — the shading has not changed.

Size — the size of the shape has not changed.

Now we can predict the second shape in the second pair.

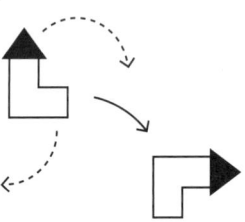

The second shape will be the first shape turned clockwise one right angle.

Now work through the possible answers to find the correct symbol.

	same shape?	*turned 90° clockwise?*
a	yes	no
b	no, a reflection	no
c	no, a reflection	no
d	yes	yes
e	yes, exactly	no

So the answer must be **d**.

Now try these

Which pattern on the right completes the second pair in the same way
as the first pair?

1 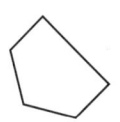 is to  as 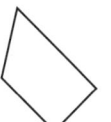 is to

   a    **b**    **c** 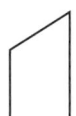   **d**    **e**

2 is to as is to

   a   **b**   **c**   **d**   **e**

3 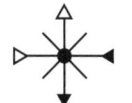 is to 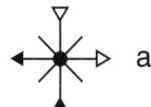 as is to

   a    **b**    **c**   **d**    **e**

4 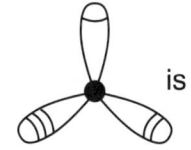 is to 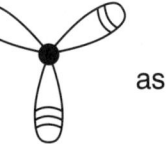 as  is to

   a 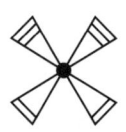   **b**    **c** 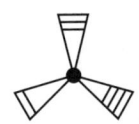   **d** 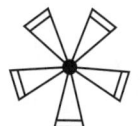   **e**

Symbols – Number

Which pattern on the right completes the second pair in the same way as the first pair?

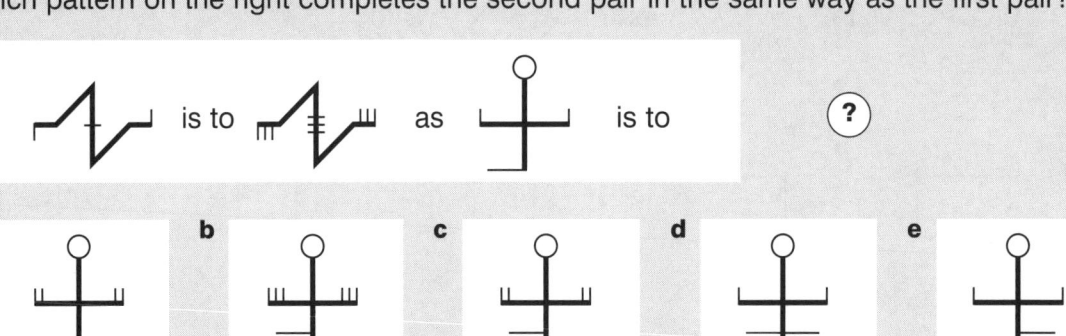

a   b   c   d   e

How to do it

Look carefully at the first pair of shapes and consider their relationship to each other.

Shape — the shape has stayed the same but has more lines on it.

Position — the position of the object has stayed the same.

Angle — the object has not been rotated.

Number — the single, thin lines on the first shape become sets of three thin lines on the second shape.

Shading — the shading stays the same.

Size — the size of the shape stays the same.

Now you can predict how the second pair is completed.

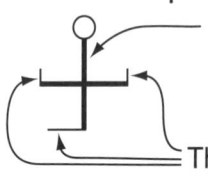

The shape, position and angle of the shape stay the same.

The single lines become sets of three lines.

The single lines become sets of three lines.

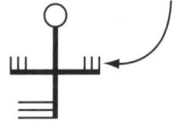

Now work through the possible answers to find the correct symbol.

	position and shape the same?	*three thin lines instead of one?*
a	yes	no
b	yes	yes
c	yes	not always
d	no, extra lines	not always
e	no, lines on wrong side	no

So the answer is **b**.

Now try these

Which pattern on the right completes the second pair in the same way as the first pair?

1   is to as is to

a 　　b 　　c 　　d 　　e

2   is to as is to

a 　　b 　　c 　　d 　　e

3  is to as  is to

a 　　b 　　c 　　d 　　e

4   is to as is to

a 　　b 　　c 　　d 　　e

75

36 Analogies

Which pattern on the right completes the second pair in the same way as the first pair?

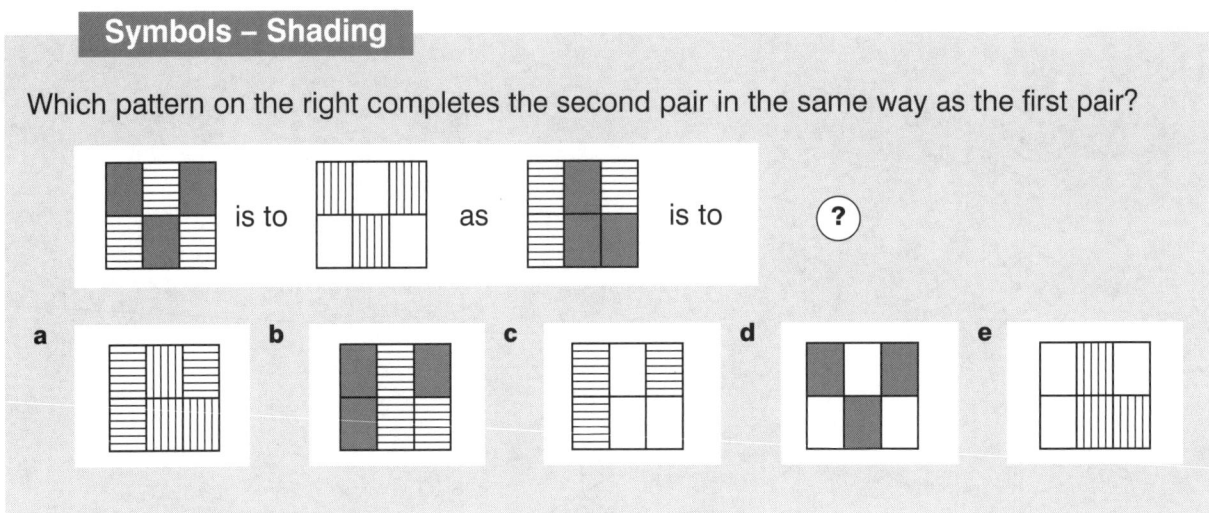

a   b   c   d   e

How to do it

Look carefully at the first pair of shapes and consider their relationship to each other.

Shape — the shapes are all the same.

Position — the shapes are all in the same position.

Angle — there is no change of angle.

Number — there is no change in number.

Shading — the shading changes as follows: black shapes become vertically-striped shapes, horizontally-striped shapes become white shapes.

Size — there is no alteration in size.

Now you can predict the second shape in the second pair. These sections will become white.

These sections will become vertically striped.

Work through the possible answers to find the correct shape.

	black has become vertically striped?	*horizontally striped has become white?*
a	yes	no
b	no	no
c	no	no
d	no	not always
e	yes	yes

So the answer must be **e**.

Now try these

Which pattern on the right completes the second pair in the same way as the first pair?

1 is to as is to

   a   **b**   **c**   **d**   **e**

2  is to  as  is to

   a    **b**    **c**    **d**    **e**

3 is to as is to

   a   **b**   **c**   **d**   **e**

4  is to  as  is to

   a    **b**    **c**    **d**   **e**

37 Analogies

Which pattern on the right completes the second pair in the same way as the first pair?

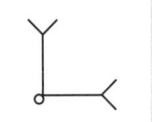 is to  as is to

a 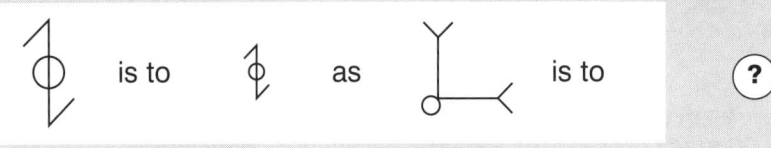 **b** **c** **d** **e**

How to do it

Look carefully at the first pair of shapes and consider their relationship to each other.

Shape — the shape is the same, but has got smaller.
Position — the shape is in the same position.
Angle — there is no change in angle.
Number — there is no change in number.
Shading — there is no shading.
Size — the second pattern is a smaller version of the first pattern.

Now you can predict the correct shape to complete the second pair.

It will be smaller than the first shape, but otherwise the same.
same shape, but smaller?
a not quite the same — some parts are smaller but others are the same
b yes
c not the same shape
d not the same shape
e some parts are smaller but not all of them
So **b** is the correct answer.

Now try these

Which pattern on the right completes the second pair in the same way as the first pair?

1

⬤ is to ⊙ as ■ is to ?

a ▫   b ■   c ▭   d ▯   e ⬠

2

is to as is to ?

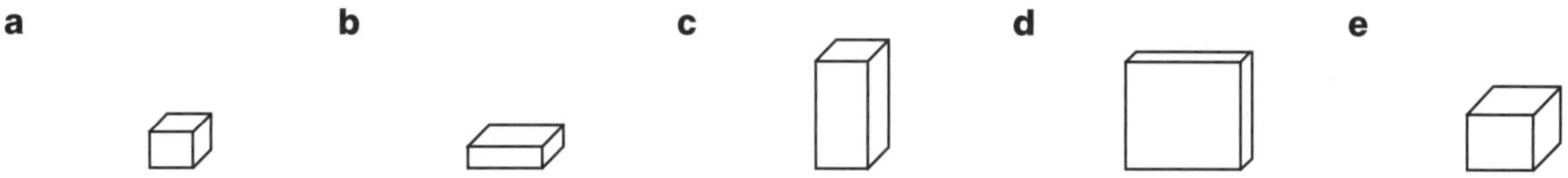

a   b   c   d   e

3

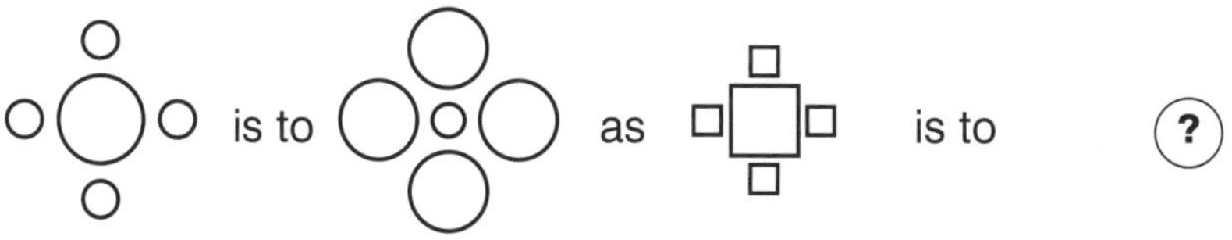

is to as is to ?

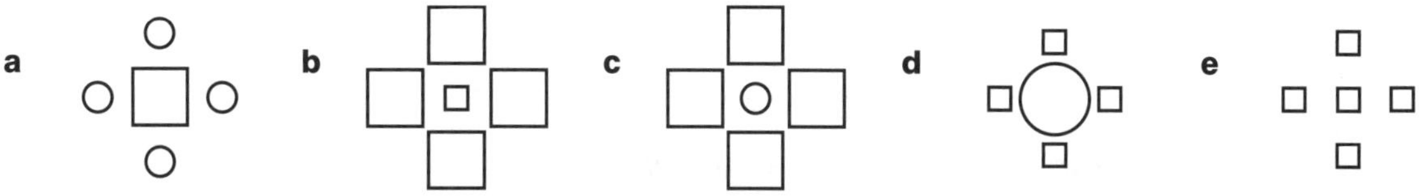

a   b   c   d   e

4

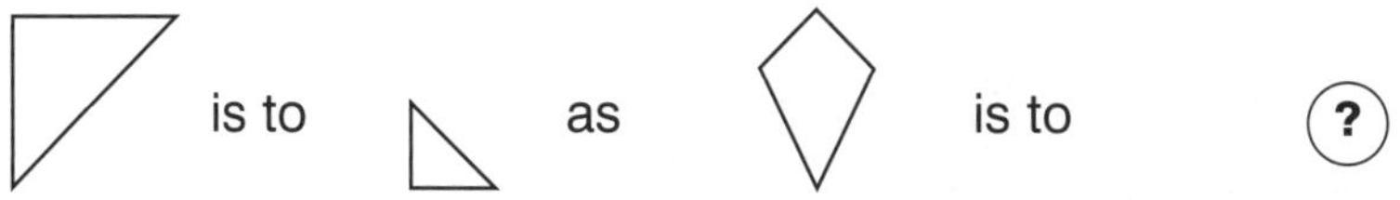

is to as is to ?

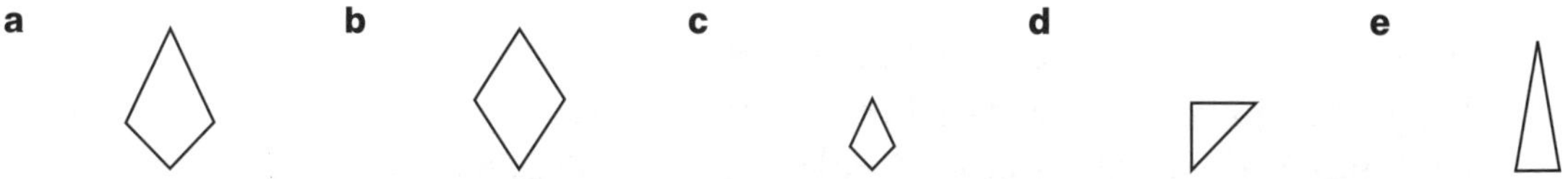

a   b   c   d   e

38 Codes

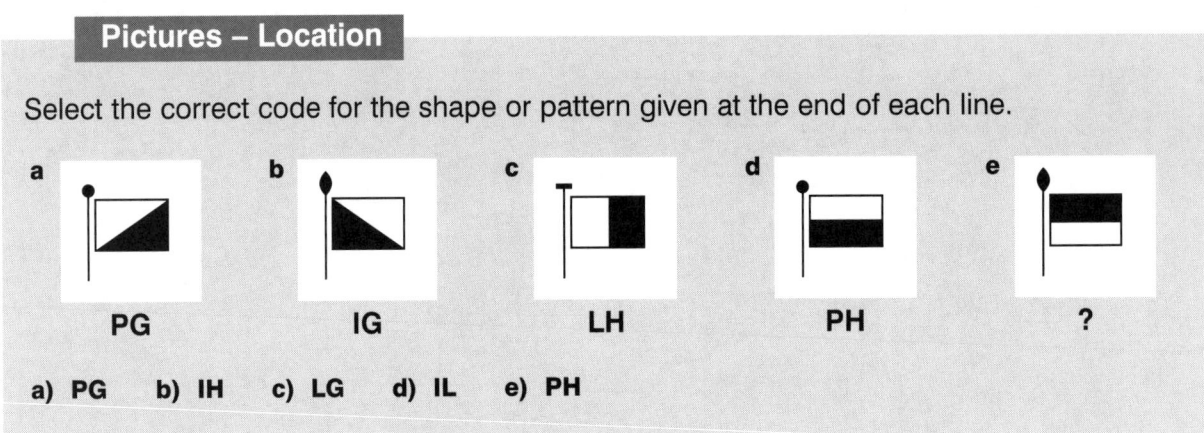

Select the correct code for the shape or pattern given at the end of each line.

a — PG
b — IG
c — LH
d — PH
e — ?

a) PG   b) IH   c) LG   d) IL   e) PH

How to do it

To work out the code you first have to look at each symbol you have been given.
Try to work out what each letter of the code is represented by in the symbol.

P — *What do the two pictures labelled **P** have in common?*

They both have
this sort of pole:

G — *What do the two pictures labelled **G** have in common?*

They both have flags
divided diagonally but
in different ways:

I — *There is only one picture with an **I**.*

It has a diagonal flag but that is
what **G** represents, so **I** must
mean this style of pole:

L — *There is only one picture with an **L**.*

It could mean the dividing line
down the middle or this style of pole:

H — *What do the two pictures labelled **H** have in common?*
They both have flags divided into rectangles.
So **L** must mean the style of pole, not the dividing line.

Now you can work out what code is correct for the pattern at the end of the line.

It has this style of pole:
This style of pole means **I.**
It has a flag divided into rectangles. This means H.

So the code for this symbol must be **IH**, which is answer **b**.

You can check what the alternative answers would mean.
PG would be a pole with a circle on top and a flag divided diagonally.
LG would be a pole with a line on top and a flag divided diagonally.
IL has codes both relating to the style of pole, so that doesn't make sense.
PH would be a pole with a circle on top and a flag divided with a straight line.

So **IH** is the only correct code.

Now try these
Select the correct code for the shape or pattern given at the end of each line.

1

| UI | RO | RI | NL | UL | ? |

a) UL b) NI c) NO d) RO e) UI

2

| AX | BY | CX | AZ | DY | ? |

a) AY b) BZ c) DX d) DZ e) CY

3

| SB | DC | DW | SC | TX | ? |

a) SX b) TC c) TB d) DX e) TW

4

| DY | AZ | BY | CY | DZ | ? |

a) BZ b) CZ c) AY d) BY e) DY

Pictures – Location

In which larger shape or pattern is the smaller shape hidden?

   a 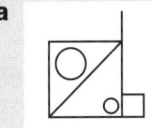   b    c 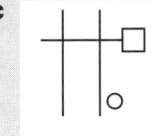   d 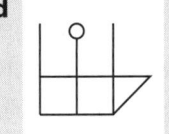   e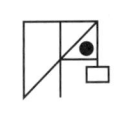

How to do it

There are two ways to solve this kind of problem.

Either:

Try to imagine 'carrying' or translating the shape given at the beginning and placing it over each of the options in turn like an overlay. Remember to turn the shape around as you try to fit it on each of the pictures, although you should not have to reflect it.

Or:

Identify a distinctive feature within the smaller shape or pattern, and use this to eliminate alternatives.

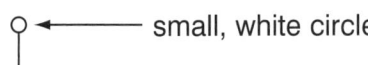 small, white circle

Do any of the options have a small, white circle?

Yes, a, c and d.

In which of these is the circle at the end of a short, straight line?

Only d.

So the answer must be **d**.

Now try these

In which larger shape or pattern is the smaller shape hidden?

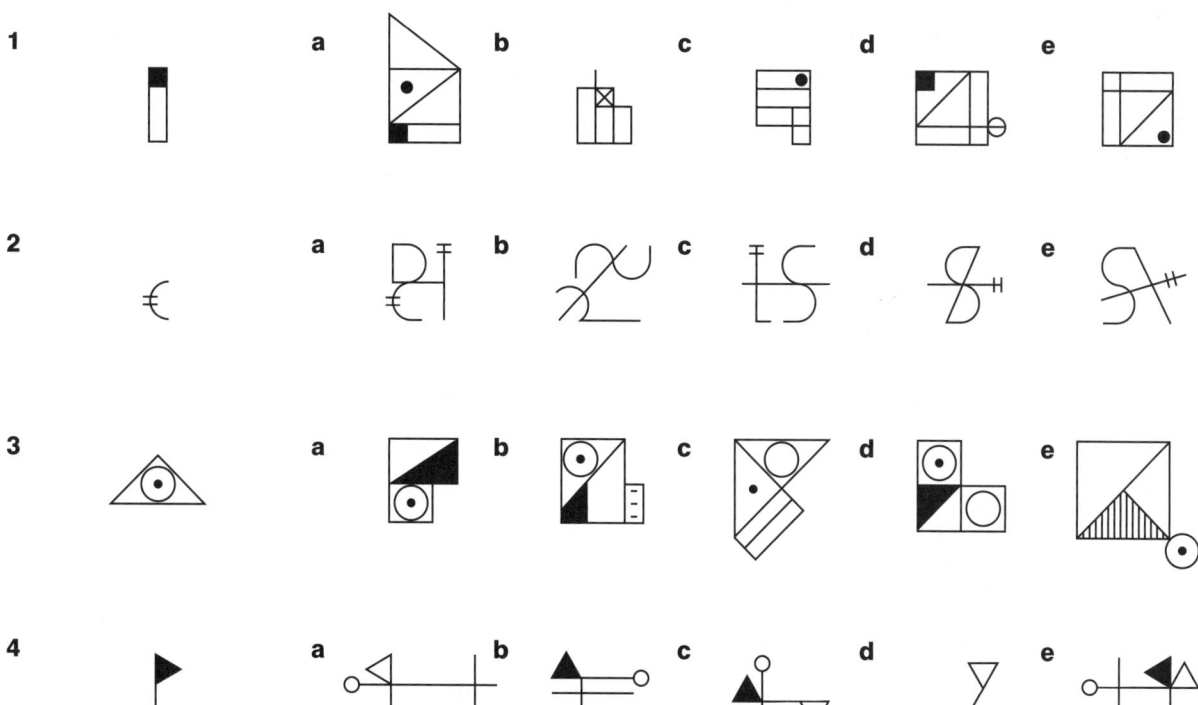

1

2

3

4

a   b   c   d   e

Pictures – Location

Which shape on the right is a reflection of the shape on the left?

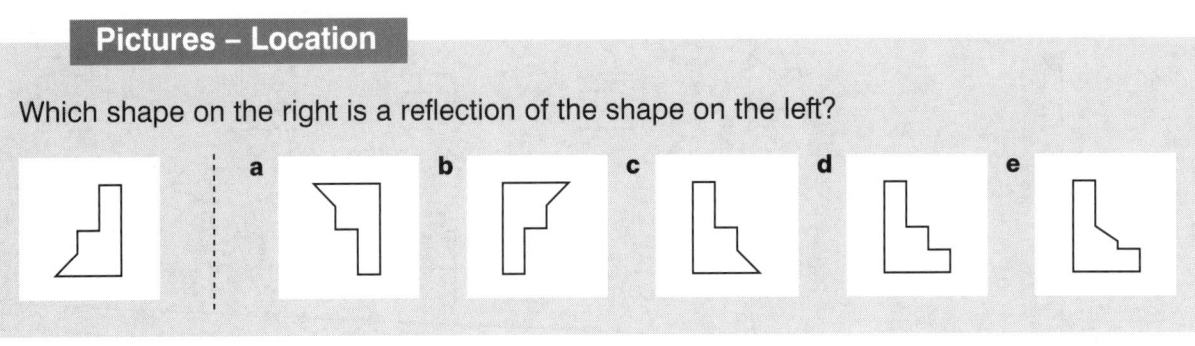

How to do it

There are different ways of finding the correct answer to these.

1. Imagine that the dotted line is a mirror line. If there was a mirror positioned there, what would the reflection of the shape look like?

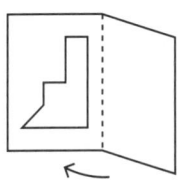 

Imagine the reflection, then match it to one of the possible answers. In this example the answer is **c**.

2. Or imagine that the dotted line is a fold line and that the pattern is drawn in wet ink. Fold and then unfold the paper along the dotted line.

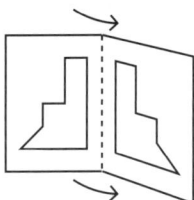

Imagine the printed shape and find it among the shapes given.

3. You may be able to 'see' the reflected shape straight away. If so, then check your answer by imagining either the mirror or the folded card.

4. If you find these methods difficult to visualise, practise using tracing paper.

   Trace the pattern carefully.

   Turn the tracing paper over.

   Match onto shapes given to find the reflected shape.

Now try these:

Which shape on the right is a reflection of the shape given on the left?

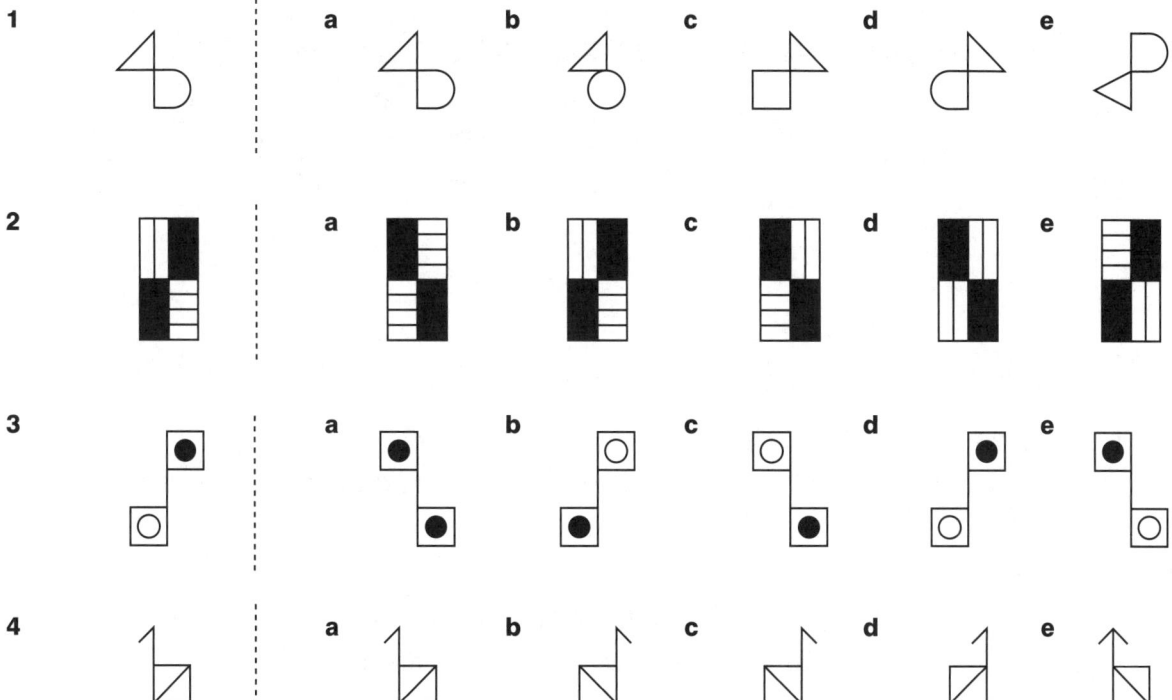

41 Nets of cubes

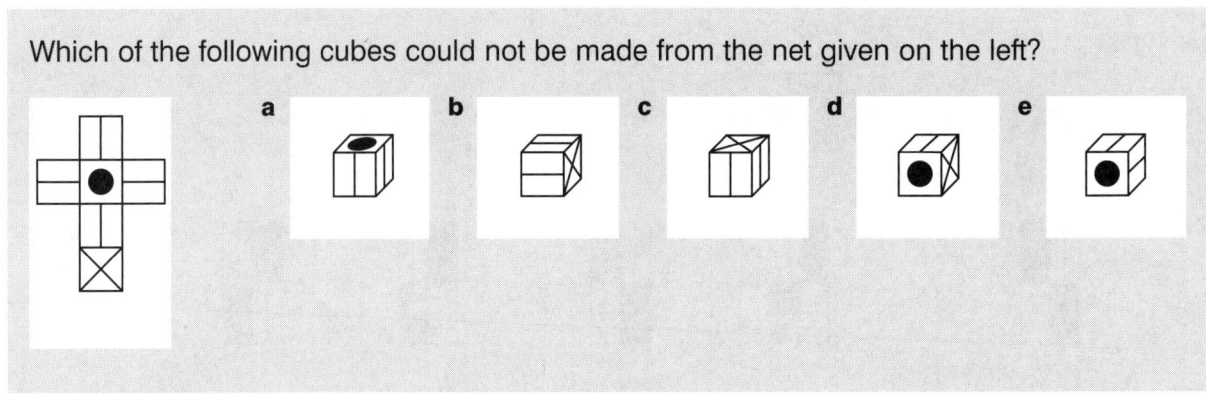

Which of the following cubes could not be made from the net given on the left?

a   **b**   **c**   **d**   **e**

How to do it

To answer these questions you have to imagine folding up the net into a cube:

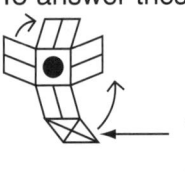

The square face at the bottom of the net
ends up opposite to the central, middle square.

Once you can imagine the net folded into a cube you can check each of the options in turn.

   a   *possible?*   **Yes.**

   b   *possible?*   **Yes.**

   c   *possible?*   **Yes.**

   d   *possible?*   **No, the dot and the cross cannot be on adjacent square faces.**

   e   *possible?*   **Yes**

d is therefore the answer.

If you have difficulty trying to visualise these, practise by cutting out paper nets and folding them into cubes.

Now try these.

Which of the following sets of cubes could not be made from the net given on the left?

1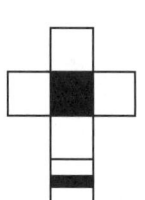
   a
   b
   c
   d
   e

2
   a
   b
   c
   d
   e

3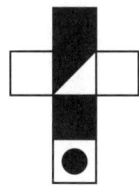
   a
   b
   c
   d
   e

4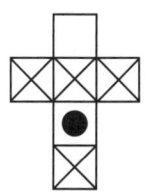
   a
   b
   c
   d
   e

Choose the shape or pattern that completes the square given.

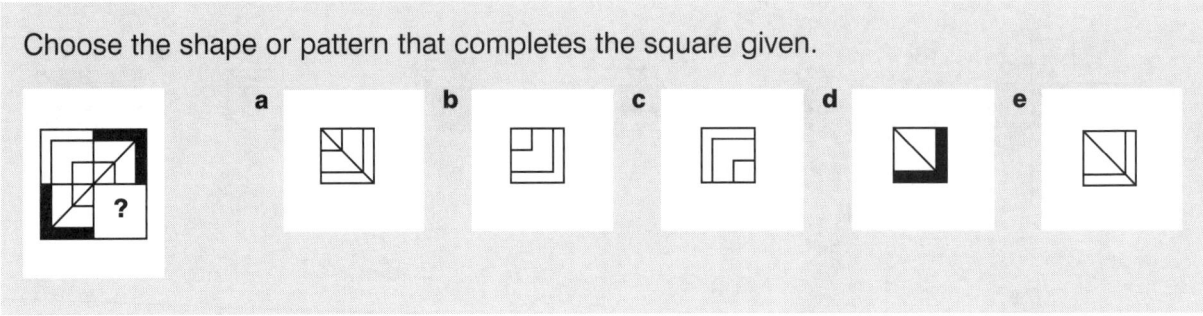

How to do it

To answer these questions you need to look very carefully at the grid given and work out how the parts are related together:

Consider: **a** *reflective symmetry*
b *rotational symmetry*
c *repeating patterns*
d *sequence*

Type a:

Is there any fold line across the grid which would make one half the reflection of the other?

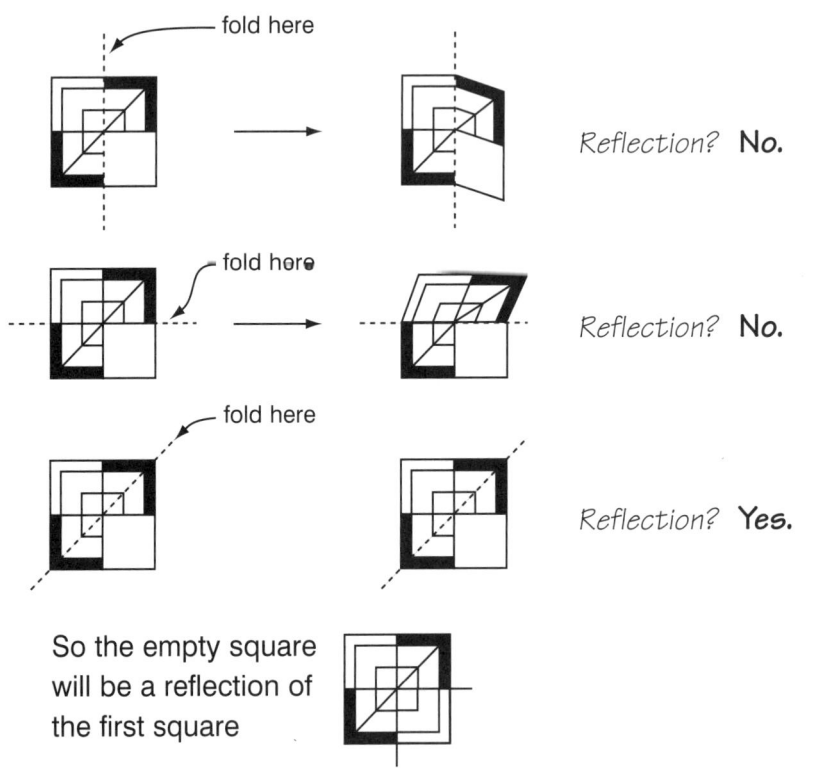

So the empty square will be a reflection of the first square

This matches choice **b**.

Now try these:
Choose the shape or pattern that completes the square given.

1 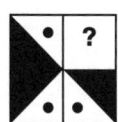   **a**   **b**   **c**   **d**   **e**

2    **a**   **b**   **c**   **d**   **e**

3 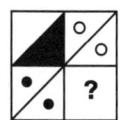   **a**   **b**   **c**   **d**   **e**

4 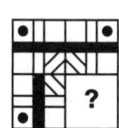   **a**   **b**   **c**   **d**   **e**

43 | Matrices

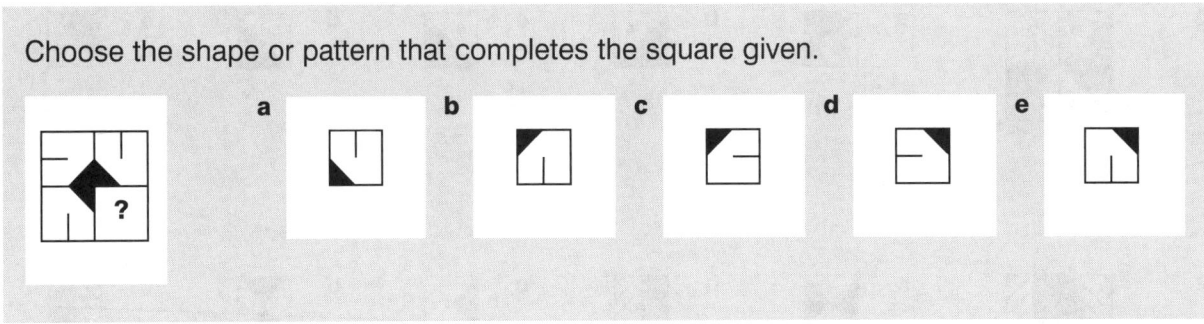

Type b:

Consider any lines of symmetry:

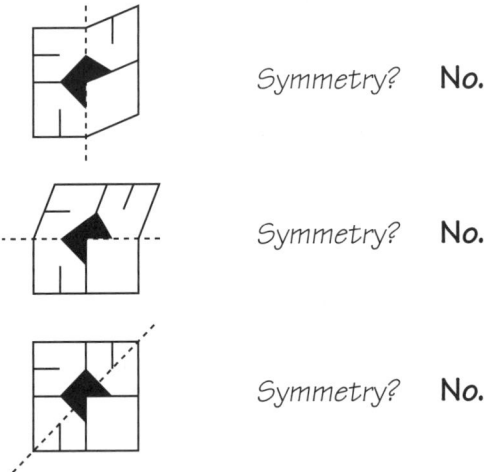

Symmetry? **No.**

Symmetry? **No.**

Symmetry? **No.**

To see if the grid has rotational symmetry imagine fixing a pin through the centre of the shape, leaving the shape free to be turned around.

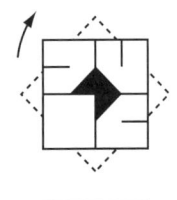

Rotate grid through 90° (one right angle). The position of the blank square has moved. The rest appear the same. The shape therefore has rotational symmetry. The missing square can be identified by looking at the bottom right square after rotation.

This matches choice **c**.

Now try these:

Choose the shape or pattern that completes the square given.

1 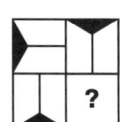   **a**   **b**   **c**   **d**   **e**

2 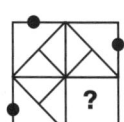   **a**   **b**   **c**   **d**   **e**

3    **a**   **b**   **c**   **d**   **e**

4 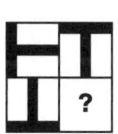   **a**   **b**   **c**   **d**   **e**

Choose the shape or pattern that completes the square given.

Type c:

Consider any lines of symmetry.

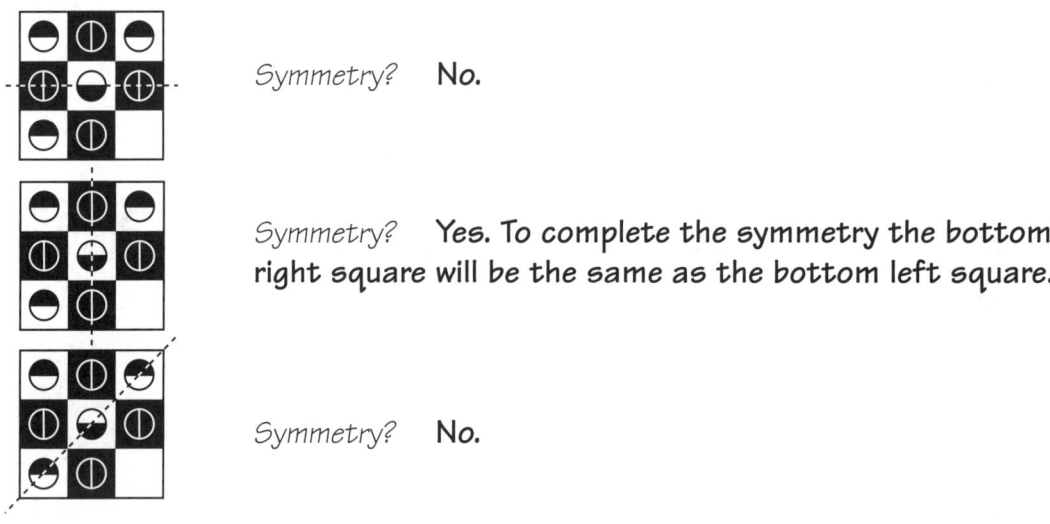

Symmetry? **No.**

Symmetry? **Yes. To complete the symmetry the bottom right square will be the same as the bottom left square.**

Symmetry? **No.**

Or consider any rotational symmetry.

The pattern on the gird is not the same at any point during the whole turn — so no rotational symmetry.

Alternatively, consider the pattern in each row:

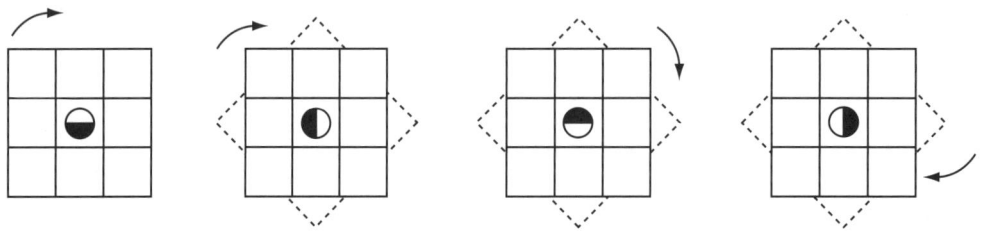

1st row   1 and 3 are the same.

2nd row   1 and 3 are the same

3rd row   3 likely to be the same as 1.

So find   as the answer.

(This can also be done considering columns instead of rows.)

So **a** is the answer.

Now try these:

Choose the shape or pattern that completes the larger square.

1 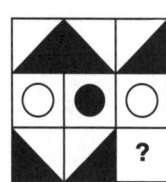 **a**   **b**   **c**   **d**   **e**

2 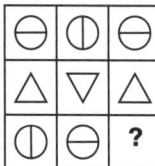 **a**   **b**   **c**   **d**   **e**

3 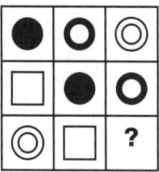 **a**   **b**   **c**   **d**   **e**

4 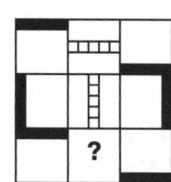 **a**   **b**   **c**   **d**   **e**

45 | Matrices

Choose the shape or pattern that completes the larger square.

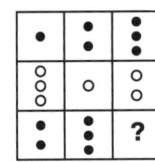

a   b   c   d   e

Type d:

Consider any line of symmetry.

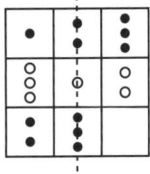
                    Symmetry?   **No.**

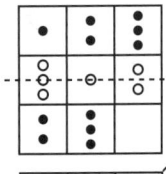
                    Symmetry?   **No.**

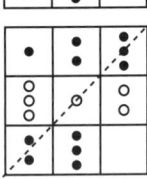
                    Symmetry?   **No.**

Or consider any rotational symmetry.

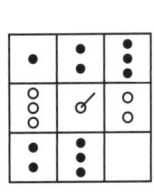 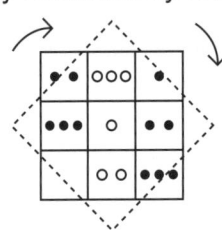 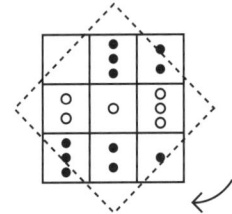 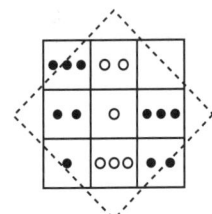

The pattern in the grid is not the same at any point during the whole turn so there is no rotational symmetry.

Or consider the sequence in each row.

1st row:	1 black dot	2 black dots	3 black dots
2nd row:	3 white dots	1 white dot	2 white dots
3rd row:	2 black dots	3 black dots	?

Pattern? **Alternate rows are black and white. 1, 2, 3 is repeated across the grid.**

The bottom right-hand square will be one black dot, which is answer **e**.

Now try these:

Choose the shape or pattern that completes the larger square.

1 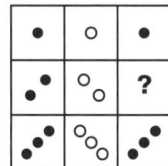　**a** 　**b** 　**c** 　**d** 　**e**

2 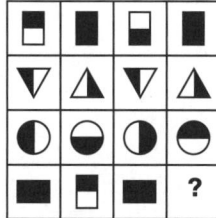　**a** 　**b** 　**c** 　**d** 　**e**

3 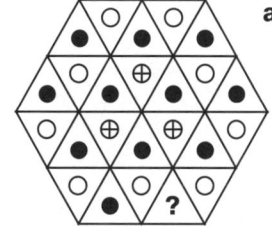　**a** 　**b** 　**c** 　**d** 　**e**

4 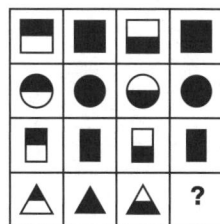　**a**　**b**　**c**　**d**　**e**

Answers

1	**1** e **2** c **3** e **4** d
2	**1** a **2** b **3** e **4** c
3	**1** d **2** e **3** c **4** d
4	**1** e **2** d **3** b **4** a
5	**1** d **2** a **3** c **4** d
6	**1** b **2** e **3** a **4** c
7	**1** c **2** b **3** d **4** b
8	**1** a **2** d **3** b **4** e
9	**1** c **2** d **3** b **4** e
10	**1** a **2** a **3** b **4** e
11	**1** c **2** c **3** e **4** a
12	**1** c **2** a **3** e **4** d
13	**1** d **2** b **3** a **4** c
14	**1** c **2** b **3** e **4** a
15	**1** d **2** b **3** c **4** a
16	**1** e **2** c **3** b **4** d
17	**1** a **2** b **3** c **4** a
18	**1** d **2** b **3** c **4** c
19	**1** d **2** a **3** d **4** c
20	**1** b **2** a **3** c **4** e
21	**1** a **2** d **3** b **4** c
22	**1** e **2** c **3** b **4** a
23	**1** e **2** c **3** e **4** b

24	**1** c **2** c **3** c **4** a **5** d **6** e
25	**1** a **2** e **3** b **4** e
26	**1** c **2** d **3** d **4** a
27	**1** d **2** c **3** b **4** a
28	**1** b **2** a **3** e **4** e
29	**1** e **2** b **3** a **4** d
30	**1** a **2** e **3** d **4** d
31	**1** c **2** a **3** d **4** e
32	**1** c **2** a **3** b **4** e
33	**1** b **2** d **3** c **4** e
34	**1** c **2** e **3** d **4** b
35	**1** e **2** b **3** a **4** e
36	**1** c **2** e **3** b **4** a
37	**1** a **2** b **3** b **4** c
38	**1** c **2** d **3** e **4** c
39	**1** a **2** a **3** b **4** c
40	**1** d **2** c **3** e **4** b
41	**1** e **2** c **3** e **4** a
42	**1** c **2** a **3** e **4** b
43	**1** c **2** e **3** d **4** c
44	**1** b **2** a **3** a **4** c
45	**1** d **2** d **3** b **4** a